THE MONSTER KIDS' JOKE BOOK

THE MONSTER KIDS' JOKE BOOK

Yet another collection of hopelessly corny,
utterly pointless jokes that you will
absolutely love to pieces!

Collected and Illustrated by

Peter Coupe

ARCTURUS PUBLISHING LIMITED, LONDON, ENGLAND

Published by Arcturus Publishing Limited
for Index
Unit 1
Henson Way
Kettering
Northants
NN16 8PX

This edition published 1999

Printed and bound in Finland

ISBN 1 - 900032 - 54 - 6

For Richard and Judith H

The Potter and the Geogger

Contents...

School Stuff...

What do you call someone who greets you
at the school door every morning?

Matt!

Teacher - Blenkinsop - Give me a sentence with the word detention in it !

Blenkinsop - I had to leave the horror film before it had finished, because I couldn't stand detention !

Head - Why haven't you been in school for the last two weeks ?

Pupil - It's not my fault - whenever I get to the road outside the school I'm never allowed to cross!

Head - Why aren't you allowed to cross ?

Pupil - Because there is a man with a sign saying 'STOP CHILDREN CROSSING!'

Fred - YUK! These school dinners taste of soap!

Freda - Well, at least you know the kitchens are clean!

Where would you find giant snails...?

...at the end of giant's fingers !

5 good reasons to go to school...

1   Even school dinners are better than my dad's.

2   The heating goes off at home at 9 o'clock.

3   You learn to be independent -
       by doing as you're told!

4   The video shop doesn't open 'til 4 o'clock!

5   You learn what life will be like when you are old
       and grumpy - by watching the teachers at
       coffee break.

Blenkinsop - Sir, my parents want me to tell you that
they were really pleased with my last report.

Teacher -   But I said you were a
complete idiot ?

Blenkinsop - But it's the first time
anyone in our family has been
really good at something!

Head - What do think about in the school holidays ?

Pupil - I never think about schoolwork !

Head - Not really much of a change for you then ?

Head - Mr Snurge, why have you put the school orchestra into the school freezer ?

Mr Snurge - They said they wanted to play some music that was a little more cool !?

For tonight's homework I want you to write
an essay on a goldfish.

I can't do that Sir !

Why on earth not ?

**I don't have any
waterproof ink !**

I'm not really interested in maths - I just go along to the lesson to make up the numbers!

★

Teacher -   Name a bird that doesn't build its own nest.

Blenkinsop - The Cuckoo.

Teacher -   That' right - how on earth did you know that ?

Blenkinsop - Everyone knows that Cuckoos live in clocks!

Did you hear about...

The P.E. teacher who used
to run round the exam room
in the hope of jogging
pupils memories ?

The maths teacher and **the
art teacher** who used to
go out together painting
by numbers ?

The craft teacher who
used to have the class in
stitches ?

The science teacher who
was scared of little glass
dishes - he was petrified ?

The cookery teacher who
thought Hamlet was an
omelette served
with bacon ?

Why did the school canteen hire a dentist ?

To make more filling meals !

★

I banged my head on my locker door this morning !

Have you seen the school nurse ?

No, just stars !

Head - Why were you sent out of the tennis class today ?

Pupil - For making a racket !

What exams do farmyard animals take ?

Hay levels !

Teacher - Blenkinsop , If
five cats were on
a bus and one get off,
how many would be left ?

Blenkinsop - None, sir !

Teacher - How do you get
that answer ?

**Blenkinsop - Because the
other 4 were copycats !**

★

Teacher - Who can tell me
which sea creature eats its
prey two at a time ?

Pupil - Noah's Shark !

15

Which of Shakespeare's plays was about a bacon factory?

Hamlet!

What's the difference between a bird watcher and a teenager?

One gets a hide and spots, the other gets a spot and hides!

Why is Frankenstein's monster rubbish at school?

He hasn't got the brains he was born with!

Teacher - Smith, what were people wearing during the Great Fire of London ?

Smith - Blazers, smoking jackets and hose ?

What is a good pet for small children ?

A Rattlesnake ??

Why were ancient sailing ships more eco-friendly ?

Because they could go for hundreds of miles to the galleon !

Teacher - Smith, I do wish you would pay a little attention !

Smith - I'm paying as little as I can, sir !

★

Teacher - Did you find the exam questions easy ?

Pupil - Oh, yes I found the question all right, it's the answers I couldn't find !

★

Why does our robot games teacher never get sick ?

Because he has a cast iron constitu- tion !

★

Teacher - Mary, why was no-one able to play cards on Noah's Ark ?

Mary - Because Noah stood on the deck !

Teacher - John, name me a famous religious warrior !

John - Attilla the Nun ?

Teacher - Smith, where are you from ?

Smith - London.

Teacher - Which part ?

Smith - All of me !

Teacher - Did you know that most accidents happen in the kitchen ?

Pupil - Yes, but we still have to eat them !

Teacher - Who was Thor ?

Pupil - The God who kept Thcratching hith thpot !

How do you cure lockjaw ?

Swallow a key ?

★

Teacher - If you had to multiply 1345 by 678
what would you get ?

Sarah - the wrong answer !

John - Dad, have we got a ladder ?

Dad - What do you need that for ?

John - For homework I have to write
an essay on an elephant !

English Teacher - Did anyone help you
write this poem Carol ?

Carol - No Miss.

English Teacher - Well, I'm delighted to meet
you at last Mr Shakespeare !

★

Teacher - Sid - what is a goblet ?

Sid - A baby turkey ?

★

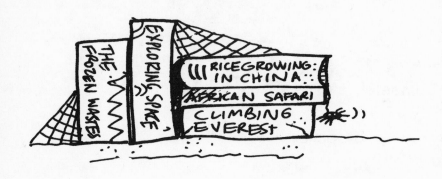

★ NEW BOOKS IN THE GEOGRAPHY LIBRARY ★

RICE GROWING IN CHINA by **Paddy Fields**

AFRICAN SAFARI by **Rhoda Lion**

EXPLORING SPACE by **Honor Rocket**

THE FROZEN WASTES by **S. Keemo**

CLIMBING EVEREST by **Percy Veerance**

★

ANIMAL SCHOOL REPORTS...

Cheetah - A nice enough boy, but not to be trusted.

Leopard - Has missed a lot of classes
this year due to spots

Hyena - Seems to think that everything is a joke

Stick Insect - Never been the same since the elephant
mistook him for a pencil !

Teacher - Steven, name an ancient musical instrument.

Steven - An Anglo - saxophone ?

Teacher - Jim, what is the largest species of
mouse in the World ?

Jim - The Hippo pota - mouse !

Teacher - Sarah, what evidence is there that
smoking is harmful to the health ?

**Sarah - Well, just look what happened
to all the dragons !**

Why did the boy throw his wristwatch out
of the window in the history exam ?

He wanted to make time fly !

Teacher - Smith, why is the handwriting in your home-work book exactly the same as Blenkinsop's ?

Smith - I borrowed his pen ?!

Teacher - Why were you late for school today Carol ?

Carol - I got a flat tyre on my bicycle !

Teacher - Did you run over some broken glass ?

Carol - No, sir, there was a fork in the road !

★

Head - I want you all to be aware of the importance of punctuality !

Blenkinsop - Well, I should be alright, I get good marks in English !

Teacher – Steven, what's a computer byte ?

Steven – I didn't even know they had teeth !

Head – Have you any idea how many teachers
work at this school ?

Pupil – About a quarter of them it seems to me !

Teacher – Why were you late this morning Veronica ?

**Veronica – I squeezed the toothpaste too hard, and
it took me half an hour to get it all back
into the tube again !**

★

You have a photographic memory Blenkinsop,

it's a shame that nothing ever develops !

★

Teacher - Jarvis, tell me a sentence with the word counterfeit in it.

Jarvis - I wasn't sure if she was a centipede or a millipede so I had to count her feet !

★

Computer Teacher - Smith, give me an example of software.

Smith - A floppy hat ?

Teacher - How would you stop a cockerel waking you at 5 a.m. ?

Pupil - Eat him for supper before you go to bed !

The Deputy Head is a funny chap,
who creeps from class to class,
he has a face that could curdle cream
and a voice like broken glass !

Teacher - Blenkinsop, How would you discover what life in Ancient Egypt was really like ?

Blenkinsop - I'd ask my Mummy !

What's the difference between a school
and a headmaster's car?

One breaks up, the other breaks down!

Teacher - What's the difference between a
horse and an elephant?

Pupil - A horse doesn't look like an elephant!

A bottle of lemonade went to teacher training college
what subject was he going to teach?

Fizzical education!

A butterfly went to teacher training college -
what subject was she going to teach?

Moth - a - matics!

★

Teacher - Who discovered Pluto?

Pupil - Walt Disney?

★

Pupil - Ugh! There's a fly in my soup!

**Kitchen assistant - Don't worry, the spider
on your bread will get it!**

★

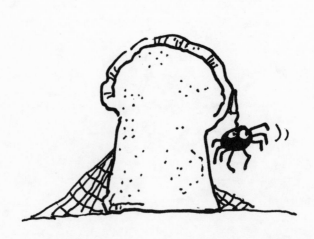

Blenkinsop , what do birds eat for their breakfast ?

Tweet - a - bix ?!

Did you hear about the music teacher who kept forgetting her register !?

We love our school
We really do
We love our lessons
Teachers too!

We love the exams
and the tricky tests
We love the school dinners
and the P.E. vests !

But why do I sound
so cheerful today
Because we just started
the Summer holiday !!

Teacher - Have you been an idiot all your life ?

Pupil - No, not yet !

What do you call the German teacher who goes to school on a motor bike ?

Helmut !

Why are teachers like doctors ?

Because they are both good at examinations !

Crazy Names...

What do you call a man who owns a seaside sweet factory?

Rock!

★

What do you call a man
with a sack, a long
white beard and a
sleigh ?

Bjorn, the oldest
postman in Iceland !

★

What do you call a monkey who is King of the jungle ?

Henry the Ape !

★

What do you call a woman with a shotgun in her hand ?

Whatever she tells you to, or else !

★

What do you call a woman who laughs as
she drives her car ?

Minnie Ha Ha !

What do you call a glove puppet
that sweeps chimneys ?

Sooty !

What name do you give a dog
that likes to wander off all the time ?

Rover !

What do you call a man
who owns a seaside
sweet factory ?

Rock !

What do you call a
woman with a frog on her head ?

Lily !

What do you call a man who lives in Scotland?

Glen!

What do you call the Roman Emperor who kept pet mice?

Julius Cheeser!

What do you call a man with a horse's head?

Nathan!

What do you call a woman who sells parrots?

Polly!

What do you call a woman who was eaten
by her cannibal husband ?

Henrietta !

★

What was the name of the man who designed King
Arthur's round table ?

Sir Cumference !

★

What do you call a man with a
car number plate on his head ?
Reg !

What do you call a man with his head in the oven ?

Stew !

What do you call an Ancient Egyptian
with no teeth ?

A Gummy Mummy !

What do you call a man with a tissue paper head ?

Russell !

What do you call a man with a
speedometer
on his head ?

Miles !

What do you call a failed lion tamer ?

Claude Bottom !

What do you call a frightened man ?

Hugo First !

What do you call a man with
a bowl of
porridge on his head ?

Scott !

What do you call a man with
an oil well on his head ?

Derek !

What do you call a girl with a bag of chips?

Anita!

What do you call a woman with
a plant pot on her head?

Rose!

What do you call a man who lifts
cars up in a garage?

Jack!

What do you call a woman
who keeps horses?

GiGi!

What do you call a man with
very strong spectacles?

Seymore !

What do you call a man who dances with
bells round his ankles ?

Maurice !

What do you call a woman with a
cash register on her head ?

Tilly !

What do you call a man with a
stolen safe on his head ?

Robin Banks !

What do you call a dog that is a always
rushing about ?

A dash-hound !

★

What do you call a rodent that likes to sword fence ?

A Mouseketeer !

★

What do you call a man who delivers
Christmas presents to lions and tigers ?

Santa Claws !

★

What do you call a man who doesn't sink ?

Bob !

★

What do you call a woman who knows
where she lives ?

Olivia !

★

What do you call the super heroes
who got run over ?

Flatman and Ribbon !

What do you call the illness that martial arts experts catch ?

Kung Flu !

What do you call a man with a computer on his head ?

Mac !

What do you call a man with a duck on his head ?

Donald !

What do you call a woman who works at the zoo ?

Ellie Fant !

What do you call a man with
horses on his head ?

Jim Karna !

What do you call a woman with a ball of
wool on her head ?

Barbara Black Sheep !

What did the Spaniard call his first
and only son ?

Juan !

What do you call a man with a vaulting horse on his
head ?

Jim !

What do you call a girl who
comes out
very early in the morning ?

Dawn !

What do you call a girl with
cakes on her head ?

Bunty !

What do you call a man with money on his head ?

Bill !

What do you call a boy with an
arm and a leg on his head ?

Hand - toe - knee !

What do you call a man with a small pig on his head?

Hamlet!

What do you call a woman who plays snooker with a pint of beer on her head?

Beatrix Potter!

What do you call a man with a male cat on his head?

Tom!

What do you call a man with
a castle on his head ?

Fort William !

What do you call a man with a box of
treasure on his head ?

Chester !

What do you call a woman with a
sinking ship on her head ?

Mandy Lifeboats !

What do you call a woman with a
pyramid on her head ?

Mummy !

What do you call a man with a
police car on his head ?

Nick, nick, nick...!

What do you call a man with a wooden head ?

Edward !

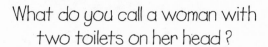

What do you call a woman with
two toilets on her head ?

Lulu !

What do you call a girl with a
head made of sugar ?

Candy !

What do you call a girl with
a head made of glass ?

Crystal !

What do you call a girl with a
head made of honey ?

Bee - trix !

What do you call a man with
legal documents on his head ?

Will !

What do you call a man with a
jumbo jet parked on his head ?

Ron Way !

What do you call a man with a steering wheel and
gearstick on his head ?

Morris !

And what do you call his son ?

Morris Minor !

What do you call a woman with
a boat tied up to her head ?

Maude !

What do you call a woman with a
tub of butter on her head?

Marge!

★

What do you call a lion with toothache?

Rory!

What do you call a man with an
anvil on his head?

Smith!

What do you call a man with a
heavy good vehicle on his head ?

Laurie !

★

What do you call a dog that's
always snapping at people ?

Camera !

★

What do you call a criminal with
a fish down his trousers ?

The Codfather !

What do you call a girl with a bucket
and spade on her head ?

Sandy !

What do you call a girl with an
orange on her head ?

Clementine !

What do you call a girl with a chimney
on her head ?

Ruth !

What do you call a man with
a pile of hay on his head ?

Rick !

What do you call a man with
turf on his head ?

Pete !

What do you call a man with a school
register on his head ?

Mark !

What do you call a girl with
flowers
growing out of her head?

Daisy!

(The girl with the beauty
spot!)

What do you call a man with a
vegetable patch
on his head?

Mr Bean!

What do you call a woman with a
badly fitted head?

Lucy!

★

What do you call a play acted by ghosts ?

A Phantomime !

What do you call a Scottish lunchtime assistant ?

Dinner Ken !

What do you call the ghost that
haunts TV chat shows ?

The Phantom of the Oprah !

What do you call a man with a
road map on his head ?

Miles !

What do you call a woman with a kettle on her head ?

Polly !
(well, in the nursery rhyme
Polly put the kettle on ?!)

What do you a man with a pair of
spectacles on his head ?

Luke !

What do you call a woman with a
doll on her head ?

Sindy !

What do you call a man with a
sprig of holly on his head ?

Buddy !

What do you call a man with a large
fiery planet on his head ?

Sunny !

What do you call a woman with some
thin paper and a pencil on her head ?

Tracey !

What do you call a woman with
half a lizard on her head?

Liz!

What do you call a man with a used
postage stamp on his head?

Frank!

What do you call a man with a policeman on his head?

Bobby!

What do you call a woman
with a plate of
food on her head?

Amelia!

What do you call a vampire with
a calculator on his head ?

The Count !

What do you call a man with some
cheese on his head ?

Gordon Zola !

What do you call a man with a
bear on his head ?

Teddy !

What do you call a woman with a
steering wheel on her head ?

Carmen !

What do you call a teacher with
a joke book on his head?

A Tee-Hee-Cher!

What do you call a man with a
pile of chopped firewood on his head?

Axel!

What do you call a man with
a mortgage offer stapled to
his head?

The Loan Arranger!

Animal
Madness...

What sweet do lambs like best ?

A big baaaaa of chocolate !

On Christmas Eve a married couple were looking up into the sky at something travelling towards them.

Is it a snow storm ?, asked the wife

No, it looks like reindeer, replied the husband.

What do you do if an elephant sits in front of you at the cinema ?

Miss the film !

What did the Pink Panther say when he stood on an ant ?

Dead ant, dead ant, dead ant dead ant dead ant...

What do elephants take to help them sleep ?

Trunkquilisers !

Where do tadpoles change into frogs ?

In the croakroom !

What did the dog say when it sat on some sandpaper ?

Ruff !

What do you call a delinquent octopus ?

A crazy, mixed -up squid !

What is the most cowardly farmyard creature ?

The Chicken !

What is the cheapest way to hire a horse ?

Stand it on four bricks !

What is the tallest yellow flower in the World ?

A Giraffodil !

What sort of bird steals from banks ?

A Robin !

What is green and white and hops ?

An escaping frog sandwich !

Why is an elephant like a teacher ?

Put a tack on an elephants chair
and you'll soon find out !

What do you call a stupid elephant with his own aeroplane ?

A Dumbo Jet !

Mary had a little lamb
the lamb began to tease her
'Stop it', she said,; the lamb refused
and now it's in the freezer !

★

When Mary had a little lamb
the doctor was surprised
but when old MacDonald had a farm
he couldn't believe his eyes

Why did the chicken blush ?

Because it saw the salad dressing !

What sort of animal does a ghost ride ?

A night mare !

How do ducks play tennis ?

With a quacket !

What do you get if you cross a hunting dog with a
newspaper writer ?

A newshound !

★

What do you call a large grey animal that's
just eaten a ton of beans ?

A smellyphant !

★

Why do bears have fur coats ?

Because they can't get plastic macs in their size !

Where is the hottest place in the jungle ?

Under a gorilla !

Two cows were talking in a field....

First Cow - Are you worried about catching this mad cow disease ?

Second Cow - Baaaa !

What is big and grey and good at sums ?

An elephant with a calculator !

Why did the chicken run out onto the football pitch ?

Because the referee whistled for a fowl !

Where do horses sit when they go to the theatre ?

In the stalls !

Why did the chicken cross the playground ?

To get to the other slide !

What ballet stars pigs ?

Swine Lake !

What do you do with a green elephant ?

Wait until he's ripe !

Why don't elephants eat penguins ?

They can't get the wrappers off !

What do sheep use to get clean ?

A Baaaa of soap !

What happened to the frog's car when it broke down ?

It was toad away !

★

What do you get if you cross a
crazy dog and a sheep ?

Baaaarrking mad !

★

Which is the trendy horse ?

The one with the pony tail !

What says Moo, Baaa, Woof, Quack, Meeooow, Oink ?

A sheep that speaks foreign languages !

Which animals with a cold do the police use ?

Sniffer dogs !

Where would you find a martian
milking a cow ?

In the milky way !

★

What is the best way to get in touch with a fish ?

Drop him a line !

Good morning Mr Butcher - do you have pigs' trotters ?

No, I always walk like this !

What do you get if you cross a pig with a millipede ?

Bacon with legs !

Where do rabbits learn to fly helicopters ?

In the hare force !

Why can't I get the King of the jungle
on the telephone ?

Because the lion is busy !

What was the name of the woman who crossed the
Gobi desert on a dromedary ?

Rhoda Camel !

★

Why does a Flamingo lift up one leg ?

Because if it lifted them both up it would fall down !

What grows down as it grows up ?

A Goose !

Where would you hear fowl language on a farm ?

Outside the chicken coop !

My mum and dad said my new boyfriend isn't fit to live with pigs !

What did you say to that ?

I stuck up for him, I said of course he is !

Why do elephants have trunks?

Because they would never fit their huge clothes into a suitcase!

When do lions have twelve feet?

When there are three of them!

First leopard - **Hey, is that a jogger over there?**

Second leopard - **Yes, great, I love fast food!**

Johnny - Mum, is our dog metric ?

Mum - Why do you ask ?

Johnny - Because Dad said it has just had a litre of puppies ?!

What is round, brown, smelly and plays music ?

A cowpat on a record player !

When do you know you have chicken pox ?

When you are constantly feeling peckish !

What is black and white and gets
complaints from all the neighbours ?

A Zebra learning to play the drums !

How can you get eggs without chickens ?

By keeping geese and ducks !

Why should you be naughty if you have
a cow for a teacher ?

**Because if you are good you might
get a pat on the head !**

I've lost my dog !!

Why don't you put a card in the
post office window ?

Don't be stupid - he can't read !

What is a polygon ?

An escaped parrot !

Where do cows go for their holidays ?

Moo York

or

Patagonia

or

Uddersfield !

Who cuts a sheep's hair ?

The Baaarber !

★

Where do farm animals keep their savings?

In a Piggy bank!

★

What is it called when a cat falls from the farmhouse roof and smashes all the glass in the greenhouse?

A Catastrophe!

First goldfish –   I told you we'd be famous one day –
                    and now it's going to come true!

Second goldfish –   Wow! When is all this going
                    to happen?

First goldfish –   They're putting us on the television
                    tomorrow!

What do you call an insect that has
forgotten the words?

A Humbug!

Why do octopuses never get mugged?

Because they are always well armed!

What do pussy cats read with their mice crispies?

Mewspapers!

If spiders live in Crawley and bees live in Hastings,
where do hares live?

On your head!

What did the idiot call his pet zebra ?

Spot !

How do frogs send messages to each other ?

Morse Toad !

What game do skunks play ?

Ping Pong !

What was the first motorised vegetable called?

The Horseless Cabbage!

I'd like a pair of gloves for my dog, please.

What breed is he?

A Boxer!

What do cows eat for breakfast?

Moosli!

Why are cows rubbish at maths ?

Because they haven't invented the cowculator yet !

What television channel do wasps watch ?

The Beee Beee Ceee !

Why do some animals wear cowboy boots in the jungle ?

Because they go lion dancing !

★

Where are all the aspirins in the jungle?

There aren't any - the paracetamol!

What was the 30 metre tall Monopoly box
doing in the jungle?

It was a big game hunter!

What do country and western singers
wear in the jungle?

Rhino-stones!

What is the first thing Tarzan puts on in the morning ?

His jungle pants !

What were Tarzan's last words ?

Who put grease on this vine ?!

Why don't leopards bother to cheat in exams ?

Because they know that they will always be spotted !

Why was the zebra put in charge of the jungle army ?

Because he had the most stripes !

What is smelly and has no sense of humour ?

A dead hyena !

What do you call a well dressed jungle cat ?

A dandy lion !

Where does a horse stay on holiday ?

In the bridle suite !

What is cold, furry and minty ?

A Polo Bear !

Where would you find a 10,000 year old cow ?

In a Moooseum !

What sort of sheep stick to the bottom of boats >

Baaaaanacles !

★

As sheep don't have money, how do they buy and sell ?

They have a baaarter system !

Why did the sheep buy a hotel ?

He's always wanted to own a baaa !

What sweet thing do sheep like best ?

Chocolate baaaaars !

What do cows put on in the morning ?

Udder pants !

How do you control a horse ?

Bit by bit !

Why was the young horse sent out of the classroom ?

He was acting the foal !

Doctor, doctor, I'm turning into a young cat !

You must be kitten me !

What sort of jokes do chickens like best ?

Corny ones !

(which is why we sell so many copies
of this book to chickens !)

Why do cats always finish the job ?

Because they purr - severe !

Where do cats go when they die ?

The Purrr - ly gates !

Where do rodents go for holidays ?

Hamster Dam !

★

What was the name of the horse that fought windmills ?

Donkey Oatey !

What sort of music do you hear most in the jungle ?

Snake, rattle and roll !

How can you travel through the jungle at
60 miles an hour ?

Inside a cheetah !

★

What do Tigers use to wake up in the morning ?

A Llama clock !

★

What is the difference between a buffalo and a bison ?

You can't wash your face in a buffalo !

★

What sort of flowers do monkeys grow ?

Chimp - pansies !

★

When cows play football, who has the whistle ?

The Heiferee !

Why don't farmers allow sheep to learn karate ?

Because their chops would be too hard !

What do you get if you cross a tortoise with a bird ?

A Turtle dove !

What was the name of the famous French cow painter ?

Too moos Lautrec !

★

What does a sheep call members of his family ?

Sheepskin !

How do you know when a dog has been naughty ?

It leaves a little poodle on the carpet !

What do you call an electronic dog ?

An Interpet !

Why don't elephants use computers ?

Because they are scared of the mouse !

EEK!

If you give a mouse gorgonzola
cheese what will happen ?

Your computer will smell !

Why did the pony keep coughing ?

He was a little hoarse !

What do sheep do on sunny days ?

Have a baa baa cue !

My daughter took her pet sheep to
the local sports day. '
Is he a good jumper ?,' someone asked her.
'Not yet,' she replied !

Why don't cows sunbathe ?

Because they don't want to tan their hides !

Why did the astronaut jump onto the cows back ?

He wanted to be the first man on the Moo !

What do they call it when an insect kills itself ?

Insecticide !

What do you get if you cross a baby with a porcupine ?

A lot of problems chang-
ing
nappies !

Why did the idiot take salt and vinegar to the zoo ?

To put on the chip-
popotamus !

What do you call an elephant that's also a witch doctor ?

A Mumbo - Jumbo !

Why are elephants such bad dancers ?

Because they have two left feet !

Why do bat mums and dads always
complain about their kids ?

Because all they do is hang around all day !

What did the Boa-constrictor say to the explorer ?

I've got a crush on you !

Which creature builds all the houses in the jungle ?

The Boa-constructor !

What do jungle police officers drive ?

Panda cars !

What did the first Piranha say to the second ?

I've got a bone to pick with you !

Where is it not safe to park in the jungle ?

On a double yellow lion !

What do you do if you fancy a bite in the jungle ?

Kick a lion up the backside !

★

Which bird is good at chess ?

The Rook !

Why is it hard to fool a stick insect ?

Because they always twig !

What are baby stick insects called ?

Twiglets !

Why did the stick insect go to university ?

He wanted to branch out !

Two baby skunks - called In and Out - went out for a
walk one day. In got lost, but his brother
soon found him. How ?

In - stinkt !

How would you sell a cow's home ?

You would need to find a byre !

What did the farmer say when the townie
asked him if he had any hay ?

Stacks !

What sort of music does a
gifted rodent write ?

Mouseterpieces !

Baby snake - Dad, are we poisonous ?

Dad snake - No, son, why do you ask !

Baby snake - I've just bitten my tongue !

★

What do they sell at Tarzan's takeaway ?

Finch, Chimps and mushy Bees !

What do you get if you cross a kangaroo with a kilt ?

Hop Scotch !

What is a sheep's favourite wine ?

Lambrusco !

What do you give a budgie with constipation ?

Chirrup of figs !

What kind of fish do pelicans like ?

Any kind - as long as they fit the bill !

What is sheepskin useful for ?

Keeping the sheep's inside where they belong !

What sort of wallpaper do birds like best ?

Flock !

Why do farmers keep cows ?

**Because there are no udder animals
as good at giving milk !**

How do elephants change their car wheels if they have a puncture ?

They lift it up with a jackal !

What bird is always running out of breath ?

The Puffin !

How do you stop a skunk from smelling ?

Tie a knot in his nose !

★

Knock, knock...

Knock, Knock...
Who's there ?
Carmen
Carmen who ?
Carmen to the front room and
look through the window !

Knock, knock...
Who's there ?
Mort
Mort who ?
Mort have known you would ask me that !

Knock, Knock...
Who's there ?
It's Jilly
It's Jilly who ?
It's Jilly out here - let me in !

Knock, Knock...
Who's there ?
Acton
Acton who ?
Acton stupid won't do you any good !

Knock, Knock...
Who's there ?
Barker
Barker who ?
Barker door's locked so I've come round to the front !

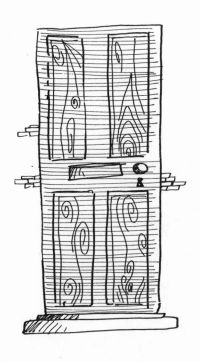

Knock, Knock...
Who's there ?
Carrie
Carrie who ?
Carrie this shopping in for
me, it weighs a ton !

Knock, Knock...
Who's there ?
Don
Don who ?
Don worry - I'm not a bur-
glar !

Knock, Knock...
Who's there ?
Eddie
Eddie who ?
Eddie minute now I'm going to sneeze !

Knock, Knock...
Who's there ?
Fred
Fred who ?
Fred you'll have to open the door to find out !

Knock, Knock...
Who's there ?
Geoff
Geoff who ?

Geoff to ask that question every single day ?

★

Knock, Knock...
Who's there ?
Harry
Harry who ?
Harry up it's just starting to rain !

Knock, Knock...
Who's there ?
Iona
Iona who ?
Iona a house just like this one !

Knock, Knock...
Who's there ?
June
June who ?
June know how long I've been waiting out here ?

Knock, Knock...
Who's there ?
Ken
Ken who ?
Ken you not guess ?

Knock, Knock...
Who's there ?
Can you Linda
Can you Linda who ?
Can you Linda me a cup of sugar ?

Knock, Knock...
Who's there ?
Mary
Mary who ?
Mary Christmas !

★

Knock, Knock...
Who's there ?
Nige
Nige who ?
Nige to see you, to see you Nige !

Knock, Knock...
Who's there ?
Oscar
Oscar who ?
Oscar nother question for goodness sake !

Knock, Knock...
Who's there ?
Pete
Pete who ?
Pete after me, 'I am going to open the door now...'

Knock, Knock...
Who's there ?
Ronnie
Ronnie who ?
Ronnie nose - need a hanky - let me in - quick !

Knock, Knock...
Who's there ?
Stella
Stella who ?
Stella same person who was here last time you asked
!

★

Knock, Knock...
Who's there ?
Tone
Tone who ?
Tone keep asking me that same old question !

★

Knock, Knock...
Who's there ?
Unger
Unger who ?
Unger the doormat is where you'll find the key !

★

Knock, Knock...
Who's there ?
Val
Val who ?
Val how am I supposed to know ?!

★

Knock, Knock...
Who's there ?
Wanda
Wanda who ?
Wanda know - open
the door and find out !

★

Knock, Knock...
Who's there ?
Xavier
Xavier who ?
Xavier anything for the
jumble sale ?

★

Knock, Knock...
Who's there ?
Annie
Annie who ?
Annie chance you'll open this door ?

Knock, Knock...
Who's there ?
Barbara
Barbara who ?
Barbara black sheep !

Knock, Knock...
Who's there ?
Carla
Carla who ?
Carla doctor, your door knocker
has just fallen off and broken my
toe !

Knock, Knock...
Who's there ?
Deb
Deb who ?
Deb better be a good reason for keeping me waiting
out here!

Knock, Knock...
Who's there ?
Emma
Emma who ?
Emma not going to tell you again !

Knock, Knock...
Who's there ?
Fanny
Fanny who ?
Fanny how you always ask that question ?!

Knock, Knock...
Who's there ?
Arthur
Arthur who ?
Arthur gotten again !

Knock, Knock...
Who's there ?
Eileen Dover
Eileen Dover who ?
Eileen Dover your fence and broke it !

Knock, Knock...
Who's there ?
Herbert
Herbert who ?
Herbert you come to the door and
see for yourself !

Knock, Knock...
Who's there ?
Morse
Morse who ?
Morse come in as quickly as possible !

Knock, Knock...
Who's there ?
Nipper
Nipper who ?
Nipper round the back and
pass my spectacles !

Knock, Knock...
Who's there ?
Oscar
Oscar who ?
Oscar a silly question...

Knock, Knock...
Who's there ?
Phil
Phil who ?
Phil this cup with sugar would you, I've just run out !

EMPTY

Knock, Knock...
Who's there ?
Quad
Quad who ?
Quad you want to know for ?

Knock, Knock...
Who's there ?
Russell
Russell who ?
Russell be home in a minute - put the kettle on !

Knock, Knock...
Who's there ?
Sandy
Sandy who ?
Sandy you living next door innit ?!

Knock, Knock...
Who's there ?
Tamara
Tamara who ?
Tamara's my birthday. Don't forget !

Knock, Knock...
Who's there ?
Urquart
Urquart who ?
Urquart just broke down, can you call the AA ?

Knock, Knock...
Who's there ?
Vera
Vera who ?
Vera long way from home and need a map !

Knock, Knock...
Who's there ?
Wendy
Wendy who ?
Wendy door finally opens you can see for yourself !

Knock, Knock...
Who's there ?
Xara
Xara who ?
Xara front door the same colour as this yesterday !

Knock, Knock...
Who's there ?
Posh
Posh who ?
Posh the door open and you'll see !

Knock, Knock...
Who's there ?
Euripides
Euripides who ?
Euripides trousers you have to buy some more !

Knock, Knock...
Who's there ?
Ben
Ben who ?
Ben down the supermarket, give us
a hand with these bags !

Knock, Knock...
Who's there ?
Clara
Clara who ?
Clara space for the shopping bags
like Ben told you to !

Knock, Knock...
Who's there ?
Lucy
Lucy who ?
Lucy Lastic !

Knock, Knock...
Who's there ?
Miguel
Miguel who ?
Miguel friends packed me in !

★

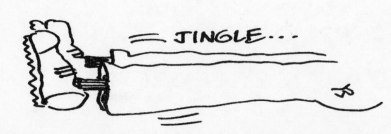

JINGLE...

Knock, Knock...
Who's there ?
Paul
Paul who ?
Paul the other one it's got bells on !

Knock, Knock...
Who's there ?
John
John who ?
John know I'm getting tired standing out here !

Knock, Knock...
Who's there ?
Atish
Atish who ?
Bless You!

Knock, Knock...
Who's there ?
Moore
Moore who ?
Moore or less the same person as before !

Knock, Knock...
Who's there ?
Carrie
Carrie who ?
Carrie this suitcase upstairs for me...

Knock, Knock...
Who's there ?
Julienne
Julienne who ?
Julienne against that front door all day ?

Knock, Knock...
Who's there ?
Carter
Carter who ?
Carter pillar !

Knock, Knock...
Who's there ?
Toulouse
Toulouse who ?
Toulouse are better than one in a
busy house I always say !

★

Knock, Knock...
Who's there ?
Double Glazing Salesman.....hello.....hello...

Knock, Knock...
Who's there ?
Furze
Furze who ?
Furze I'm concerned you can keep the door closed !

Knock, Knock...
Who's there ?
Germaine
Germaine who ?
Germaine I can't come in unless I tell you ?

Knock, Knock...
Who's there ?
Mush
Mush who ?
Mush you always ask me this ?

Knock, Knock...
Who's there ?
Hilda
Hilda who ?
Hilda 'owt for a laugh like, why aye !

Knock, Knock...
Who's there ?
Mandy
Mandy who ?
Mandy lifeboats !

Knock, Knock...
Who's there ?
Frank
Frank who ?
Frank you for asking !

Knock, Knock...
Who's there ?
Egon
Egon who ?
Egon down the shops !

Knock, Knock...
Who's there ?
Harmony
Harmony who ?
Harmony times do I have to tell you ?!

Knock, Knock...
Who's there ?
Sitter
Sitter who ?
Sitter good time to come round ?

Knock, Knock...
Who's there ?
Don
Don who ?
Don be afraid....look into
my eyes....you are feeling sleepy...

Knock, Knock...
Who's there ?
Ma
Ma who ?
Ma car broke down again !

Knock, Knock...
Who's there ?
A guest
A guest who ?
A guest you wouldn't recognise my voice !

★

Knock, Knock...
Who's there ?
Arnie
Arnie who ?
Arnie chance of coming in ?

★

Knock, Knock...
Who's there ?
Dan
Dan who ?
Dan Dan Dan Dan Daaaannnn !

★

Knock, Knock...
Who's there ?
Carrie
Carrie who ?
Carrie on like this
and I'll freeze to
death out here !

★

Knock, Knock...
Who's there ?
Hal
Hal who ?
Halloo !

Knock, Knock...
Who's there ?
A ghost
A ghost who ?
Thought it would scare you !

Knock, Knock...
Who's there ?
Kenya
Kenya who ?
Kenya please just open the door !?

★

Knock, Knock...
Who's there ?
France
France who ?
France y meeting you here !

Knock, Knock...
Who's there ?
Adolf

Adolf who ?
Adolf ball hit me in de mouf !

Knock, Knock...
Who's there ?
Chris
Chris who ?
Chris Packet, but my friends call me Russell !

Knock, Knock...
Who's there ?
Iona
Iona who ?
Iona have eyes for you !

Knock, Knock...
Who's there ?
Tinkerbell
Tinkerbell who ?
Tinkerbell would look nice on my bike !

Knock, Knock...
Who's there ?
Justin
Justin who ?
Just in time to open the door for me !

Knock, Knock...
Who's there ?
Maquis
Maquis who ?
Maquis just snapped in the lock !

Knock, Knock...
Who's there ?
Isabell
Isabell who ?
Isabell not working ?

Knock, Knock...

Who's there ?
Jethro
Jethro who ?
Jethro people out if they can't pay their bill ?

★

Knock, Knock...
Who's there ?
Amos
Amos who ?
Amosquito bit me !

★

Knock, Knock...
Who's there ?
Lettuce
Lettuce who ?
Lettuce in and you'll find out !

★

Knock, Knock...
Who's there ?
Ivor
Ivor who ?
Ivor message
for a Mr Smith ?!

★

Knock, Knock...
Who's there ?
Sid
Sid who ?
Sid down next to me !

Knock, Knock...
Who's there ?
Shirley
Shirley who ?

Shirley you know the sound of my voice by now ?

Knock, Knock...
Who's there ?
Midas
Midas who ?
Midas well open the door and find out !

★

Knock, Knock...
Who's there ?
Jester
Jester who ?
Jester minute I've forgotten !

★

Knock, Knock...
Who's there ?
Sinbad
Sinbad who ?
Sinbad condition your front door !

★

Knock, Knock...
Who's there ?
Harry
Harry who ?
Harry up and let me in !

Knock, Knock...
Who's there ?
Caine
Caine who ?
Caine you see me through the glass ?

Knock, Knock...
Who's there ?
Yul
Yul who ?
Yul find out when you open the door

Knock, Knock...
Who's there ?
Cattle
Cattle who ?
Cattle get out if you open the door,
I'll come in through the window !

Knock, Knock...
Who's there ?
And your old lady
And your old lady who ?
I didn't know you could yodel !

Knock, Knock...
Who's there ?
Doris
Doris who ?
Doris closed – that's why I'm having to knock !

Knock, Knock...
Who's there ?
Europe
Europe who ?
Europe bright and early today !

Knock, Knock...
Who's there ?
Orang
Orang who ?
Orang the doorbell but it doesn't seem to
work, so now I'm knocking !

Knock, Knock...
Who's there ?
Alf
Alf who ?
Alf feed the cat while you're on holiday !

Knock, Knock...
Who's there ?
Stephanie
Stephanie who ?
Stephanie me - who else could it be !

Knock, Knock...
Who's there ?
Witch doctor
Witch doctor who ?
The one with the long stripy scarf !

Knock, Knock...
Who's there ?
Wooden shoe
Wooden shoe who ?

Wooden shoe like to see ?
Knock, Knock...
Who's there ?

May-Belle
May-Belle who ?
May-Belle don't work either, so I'm knocking !

Knock, Knock...
Who's there ?
Noah
Noah who ?
Noah a good place to hide from this rain ?

Knock, Knock...
Who's there ?
Will
Will who ?
Will I ever get in !?

Knock, Knock...
Who's there ?
Luke
Luke who ?
Luke out - the Martians are landing !

Knock, Knock...
Who's there ?
Mindy
Mindy who ?
Mindy porch !

Knock, Knock...
Who's there ?
Othello
Othello who ?
Othello could freeze to death out here !

Knock, Knock...
Who's there ?
Fools Rachid
Fools Rachid who ?
Fools Rachid where angels fear to tread !

Knock, Knock...
Who's there ?
Oasis
Oasis who ?
Oasis, it's your brother, I forget me key !

Knock, Knock...
Who's there ?
Mickey
Mickey who ?
Mickey don't fit - have you changed the lock ?

Knock, Knock...
Who's there ?
Kong
Kong who ?
Kong ratulations you've won the lottery !

Knock, Knock...
Who's there ?
Moss
Moss who ?
Moss be time to move onto the next section !!

Monster Mirth...

What do you call a monster airline steward?

A Fright attendant!

What do monsters eat ?

Shepherds Pie
and
Ploughmans Lunch

Why are monsters always falling out
with each other ?

There's always a bone of contention !

What was the name of the monster in the 3 bears ?

Ghouldilocks !

What are a monsters favourite fairground rides ?

The Helter Skeleton !

or the

Roller Ghoster !

Which monster is the most untidy ?

The Loch Mess Monster

What songs do they play at ghostly discos ?

Haunting melodies !

What does a young monster call his parents?

Mummy and Deady!

Mum, I've decided I don't like my brother after all!

Well, just eat the chips and leave him on the side of the plate!

★

Why was the monster catching centipedes?

He wanted scrambled legs for breakfast!

What game do ghostly mice play at parties ?

Hide and Squeak !

Where do monsters live ?

Crawley !

Why did the monster buy an axe ?

Because he wanted to get ahead in life !

Why did the monster eat his music teacher ?

His Bach was worse than his bite !

Why was the monster scared of the computer ?

Because its memory had a killer bite !

What position do monsters play in football ?

They are the ghoul posts !

Why do monsters have lots of nightmares ?

They like to take their work
to bed with them !

What game do young monsters play ?

Corpse and Robbers !

What do monsters like to pour on their Sunday dinner ?

Grave - y !

Where do monster go on their American holidays ?

Death Valley !

How does Frankenstein's monster eat ?

He bolts his food down !

Why should you never touch a monster's tail ?

**Because it is the end of the monster,
and it could also be the end of you !**

Why did the monster comedian like playing to skeletons ?

Because he knew how to tickle their funny bones !

During which age did mummies live ?

The Band - Age !

Eat your sprouts,
son, they'll put
colour in your
cheeks !

But I don't want
green cheeks !

What do you call a monster that comes to
your home to collect your laundry ?

An Undie-taker !

What is the first thing a monster does
when you give him an axe ?

Writes out a chopping list !

★

Which room in your home can ghouls not enter ?

The living room !

Why did the monster have twins in his lunchbox ?

In case he fancied seconds !

What job could a young monster do ?

Chop assistant !

How did the monster cook the local hairdresser ?

On a barbercue !

What do monsters like for breakfast ?

Dreaded Wheat !

What did the metal monster have on his gravestone ?

Rust In Peace !

What do monsters have at tea time ?

Scream cakes !

What did the mummy monster say to her child at the dining table ?

Don't spook with your mouth full !

What is a young mon- sters favourite TV programme ?

BOO Peter !

Where do monsters live ?

Bury !

Why didn't the skeleton fight the monster ?

He didn't have the guts !

★

What do you call a monster airline steward ?

A fright attendant !

Why was the monster hanging round
the pond with a net ?

He was collecting the ingredients for toad in the hole !

Where do skeletons keep their money ?

In a joint account !

★

What film did the monster James Bond star in ?

Ghouldfinger !

What has 50 legs ?

A centipede cut in half !

What sort of curry do monsters make
from their victims hearts ?

Tikka !

Why did the monster have a sprinter in his lunchbox ?

He liked fast food !

Some monster holidays...

Good Fryday !
(Good for frying anyone who gets close enough to
grab !)

Eater Sunday and Eater Monday !
(Monsters don't have eggs !)

Guy Forks Night !
(Stay at home on November 5th if you are called Guy !)

Crisps and Eve !
(Another traditional monster recipe !)

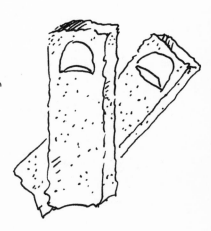

Why are monsters so horrible ?

It's in the blood !

Why do monsters breed fish with hands ?

So they can have fish fingers with their chips !

What do monsters eat if the catch someone breaking into their home ?

Beef burglers !

What do monsters make with cars ?

Traffic jam !

Why do monsters never eat police officers ?

They hate truncheon meat !

Did you hear about the monster who asked if he could leave the dining table ?

His mum said yes, she would put it in the fridge and he could eat it later !

Some foreign holiday resorts favoured by monsters...

Eat a Lee !

Belch um !

Gnaw Wayne !

Sweet Den

What do headless monsters eat ?

Chops !

What do Italian monsters eat ?

Spookgetti !

Which monster monkey thinks he can sing ?

King Song !

What do you call a monster with an
axe buried in his head ?

Nothing - it's perfectly normal for monsters !

Who patrols the graveyard at night ?

A fright watchman !

What did the policeman say to the
monster with three heads ?

Hello, hello, hello !

Barmy Brain Teasers...

Why have you buried my car?

Because the battery is dead!

What did the bull say when he came back
from the china shop ?

I've had a really smashing time !

★

When do 2 and 2 make more than 4 ?

When they make 22 !

★

Why were the naughty eggs sent out of the class ?

For playing practical yolks !

Why should you never listen too closely to the match ?

Because you might burn your ears !

Why did the bakers work late ?

Because they kneaded the dough !

How many monsters would it take to fill this room ?

No idea, I'd be off after the first one arrived !

How does Father Christmas start a joke?

This one will sleigh you...!

What jewelry do ghosts wear?

Tombstones!

What do mummies use to wash up?

Pharaoh liquid!

How can you sleep like a log ?

Put your bed in the fireplace !

What do space monster sweet shops sell ?

Mars bars, galaxy and milky way !

★

What can you catch and hold but never touch ?

Your breath !

What do you call the finest Indian wine ?

Vin - daloo !

What are dog biscuits
made from ?

Collie - flour !

What flower do you have
to keep a look out for in
the garden ?

Anenome !

SECRET
SOUP

007

VARIETIES

KEEP
OUT !

Where would you find
secret soup ?

At the minestrone of
defence !

What do you do if a ghoul rolls his eyes at you ?

Just pick them up and roll them back !

Why are you burying my car ?

Because you said the battery was dead !

Why did the man jump up and down
after taking his medicine ?

Because he forgot to shake the bottle
before he took it !

Which famous artist had a bad cold?

Vincent van cough!

Why did the bur-
glar buy a surf
board?

He wanted to start
a crime wave!

What does a toad
sit on?

A toadstool!

What does a toad
use for making
furniture?

A toad's tool!

Why don't pigs telephone one another ?

Because there is too much crackling on the line !

★

Why are pigs no good at do-it-yourself ?

Because they are ham-fisted !

★

Why did the burglar break into the music shop ?

He was after the lute !

Why did the burglar break into the bakers ?

He wanted to steal the dough !

Why did the burglar go to the bank ?

To recycle his bottles !

How do you keep a fool in suspense ?

I'll tell you tomorrow !

How do you make a fool laugh on Saturday ?

Tell him a joke on Wednesday !

Why must you never make a noise in a hospital ?

Because you don't want to wake the sleeping pills !

What is a squirrel's favourite chocolate ?

Whole nut !

Where would you find a bee ?

At the start of the alphabet !

★

Where is there always a queue ?

In between P and R !

★

What does it mean if your nose starts to run ?

It's trying to catch a cold !

★

Why is the Leopard the only animal that can't
hide from hunters ?

Because it is always spotted !

Why did the elephant refuse to play cards
with his two friends ?

**Because one of them was lion and
the other was a cheetah !**

How do you make a Venetian blind ?

Paint his spectacles black when he's asleep !

Who is a caveman's favourite band ?

The stones !

★

Why does a giraffe have such a long neck ?

Have you ever smelled a giraffe's feet !

Mary had a little fox,
it ate her little goat,
now everywhere that Mary goes,
she wears her fox-skin coat !

What jungle animal would you find at the North Pole ?

A lost one !

What sort of frog is covered in dots and dashes ?

A morse toad !

Where do cows go for history lessons ?

To a mooseum !

★

What does a polar bear use to keep his head warm ?

A polar ice cap !

What does a hard of hearing apple have in his ear ?

A lemonade !

How do plumbers get to work ?

By tube !

What sort of music do police officers like ?

Anything with a regular beat !

What do you need to electrocute
an orchestra ?

A good conductor !

Good morning Mr Butcher, do you have pig's feet ?

Certainly, sir !

Well, wear larger shoes and no-one will notice !

How do teddies like to ride horses ?

Bear back !

What do teddies take when they are
going on holiday ?

Just the bear essentials !

Who always puts thyme in his soup ?

A clockmender !

Waiter, there's a small worm in my salad !

Oh, dear, I'll tell the chef to send you a large one !

What do you give a dog for breakfast ?

Pooched eggs !

Why couldn't the orange call the apple on the telephone?

Because the lime was engaged!

Why are those clothes running out of the sports shop?

They're jogging suits!

Why do video machines always win their football matches?

Because they have fast forwards!

Why do cows lie down together when it rains ?

To keep each udder dry !

What sort of fruit would you find in a diary ?

Dates !

What do vegetarians take home for wages ?

A Celery !

Atissshhhooo, I don't feel very well !

Wow, I didn't know that having a cold affected your sense of touch !

Did you hear about the punk rocker who fell over and 50 others fell over at the same time ?

He started a chain reaction !

What do you call a man who never pays his bills ?

Owen !

What do mice sing at birthday parties ?

For cheese a jolly good fellow !

When should you put your electric guitar in the fridge ?

When you want to play some really cool music !

Where is the greenest city in Europe ?

Brussels !

★

Which Italian city is good for wandering round ?

Rome !

Which English city has the best stock of electrical connectors ?

Leeds !

Which French city has the best stock of paper ?

Rheims !

Why are bearded men fearless ?

Because they can never have a close shave !

★

What song do sweets sing at parties ?

For he's a jelly good fellow !

★

How do you write a essay on a giraffe ?

With a long ladder !

★

How do you shock people at a tea party ?

Serve current buns !

What says 'now you see me, now you don't...'

A nun on a zebra crossing !

Why do vampires like crossword puzzles ?

They like the crypt - ic clues !

My cellar is full of toadstools !

How do you know they're toadstools ?

There's not mushroom in there for anything else !

Why do some anglers suck their maggots?

So they can wait for a fish to bite with baited breath!

Should I give the dog some of my pie?

Certainly not, he didn't want it when I gave it to him earlier!

What shampoo do spooks use?

Wash - n - ghost!

What sort of ghosts haunt hospitals?

Surgical spirits!

How do you tell a ghost how lovely they are ?

'you're bootiful !'

What do you get if you cross a skunk with an owl ?

Something that stinks, but doesn't give a hoot !

What did the doctor give Cleopatra for her headache ?

An asp - irin !

What do you give a ghost with a headache?

AAAAGGGGHHHHspirin!

Where do vampires go on holiday?

Veinice!

How do you know if a bicycle is haunted?

Look for spooks in the wheels!

What do you call a doctor with a bright
green stethoscope?

Doctor!

What sort of parties do vampires like best?

Fang - cy dress parties!

Why should you never tell your secrets to a piglet ?

Because they might squeal !

How do rabbits go on holiday ?

By British hareways !

How do you talk to a hen ?

By using fowl language !

Who is the patron saint of toys ?

Saint Francis of a see-saw !

Which teacher won't allow sick notes ?

The music teacher !

What is a *juggernaut* ?

An empty jug !

What does B.C. stand for ?

Before calculators !

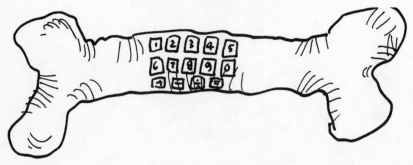

What did the stupid fencing team take to the olympics ?

5000 litres of creosote !

Which trees grow at the seaside ?

Beach trees !

★

How do you make a Mexican chilli ?

Take him to Iceland !

What do cannibals do at a wedding ?

They toast the bridge and groom !

What is a mistake ?

An unmarried female bank robber !

Why is the bookshop the tallest
building in the town ?

**Because it has the
most stories !**

Who do you ask to see if you find
a twig in your salad ?

The branch manager !

What sort of person gets paid to make faces all day ?

A clockmaker !

What happened when the vampire went insane ?

He went batty !

What sort of tree grows near a volcano ?

A lava tree !

What did the skunk say when the wind
changed direction ?

It's all coming back to me now !

Where do you find monster snails ?

On the end of monsters' fingers !

Why must you always have holes in your socks ?

**You wouldn't be able to get your feet
in them if you didn't !**

In which battle was Alexander the Great killed ?

His last one !

What is yellow, wears glasses and sings ?

'Nana Mouskouri !

In which film does fruit rule the world ?

Planet of the grapes !

Where do squirrels keep their nuts ?

In a pan-tree !

Which is the strongest day of the week ?

Sunday - all the others are weak days !

What do you call someone who can't
stop stealing carpets ?

A rug addict !

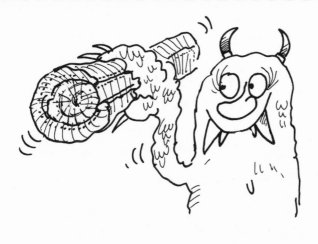

Which of these is correct -
'egg yolk is white'
'egg yolk are white'

Neither - egg yolk is yellow !

Where would you find a rubber trumpet ?

In an elastic band !

★

What goes up but never comes down ?

Your age !

Which birds fly in formation?

The Red Sparrows!

What do you call a lion with no eyes?

Lon!

Why are cars rubbish at football?

They only have one boot each!

Why did the satsuma go to the doctor ?

It wasn't peeling too good !

What music does King Neptune like ?

Sole !

Why does it snow in the Winter ?

Because it's too hot in the *Summer* !

What do you call a very old Dracula ?

Gran pire !

What sort of fish would you find in a bird cage ?

A perch !

★

What do you throw for a stick insect to fetch ?

A dog !

★

What is a vampires favourite coffee ?

Decoffinated !

★

Where do insects go to dance ?

A cricket ball !

Why is it impossible to open a locked piano lid?

Because all the keys are on the inside!

What do you get if you read the Monster Kids' Joke Book to an Oxo cube?

A laughing stock!

What runs all the way round your house
without moving ?

The fence !

What show do undertakers look forward to every
year ?

The hearse of the year show !

How do you measure the size of fruit ?

With a green gauge !

What do you get if you
leave your
teaspoon in the cup ?

**A sharp pain in the eye
when you drink !**

What has no legs, but runs across
the bathroom floor ?

Water !

Why was the blacksmith arrested ?

For forging !

What is it called when a fish tells lies in a courtroom ?

Perchery !

Why is a bad bank like a lazy schoolboy ?

They both lose interest quickly !

What should you take if you feel run down ?

The number of the car that hit you !

Which robot was stuck in road works ?

R 2 Detour !

How do hens dance ?

Chick to chick !

Did you hear about the Martian who went to a plastic surgeon for a face lift ? She wanted her face to look like a million dollars, so the surgeon made it all green and crinkly !

★

Where do Martians live ?

In greenhouses !

★

What do you give the man who has everything ?

Nothing !

★

Where would
you keep
sheep covered
in ink ?

In a pen !

What do you call a story that someone
tells you at breakfast every day ?

A cereal !

What do you call a story that someone tells you
in the car on the way to school every day ?

A mini-serial !

Who drives her children to school in a small car ?

A minimum !

What do vampires do before driving a car ?

They check the wing mirrors !

Why do vampires never marry ?

They are bat - chelors !

Why do woodworm have no friends ?

Because they are boring creatures !

Where can you go for a quick break by the beach ?

A seaside karate club !

How do you stop your nose from running ?

Take away its trainers !

What is the best thing to put in a sandwich ?

Your teeth !

Who writes joke books in never never land !

Peter Pun !

What do you get if you cut a comedian in two ?

A half wit !

★

What do you get if
you cross a bee
with an ape ?

Sting Kong !

How do jockeys
send messages to
each other ?

With horse code !

What do dogs go
to the hairdresser
for ?

A shampoodle and
setter !

Why did the cow look into the crystal ball ?

To see if there was a message from the udder side !

★

What did the doctor give the deaf fisherman ?

A herring aid !

★

Who thought up the
series 'Star Trek' ?

Some bright Spock !

★

Why couldn't the astronauts land on the moon?

Because it was full!

What time is it when astronauts are hungry?

Launch time!

How can you cook turkey that really tickles the taste buds?

Leave the feathers on!

What do they pay police officers for working late?

Copper Nitrate!

What's the special offer at the pet shop this week ?

Buy one cat - get one flea !

What do you call a bike that bites your bottom
when you try to get on it ?

A vicious cycle !

Why do demons and ghouls get on so well together ?

Because demons are a ghouls best friend !

What tool do ghostly builders use ?

A spirit level !

Why are lots of famous artists French ?

Because they were born in France !

What do you get...

What do you get if you cross a toad
with a science fiction film ?

Star warts !

What do you get if you cross a road
with a blindfold ?

Knocked down !

What do you get if you cross a mouse
with a tin opener ?

**Something that can get the cheese from the 'fridge
without even opening the door !**

What do you get if you cross a car with the millenium ?

A Rover 2000 !

What do you get if you cross a
bridge with your feet ?

To the other side !

What do you get if you cross a parrot
and a scary film ?

A bad attack of the polly-wobbles !

What do you get if you cross a car
with a row of mountains ?

A Range Rover !

What do you get if you cross a wizard
and an aeroplane ?

A flying sorcerer !

What do you get if you cross a
plant pot and an infant ?

A growing child !

What do you get if you cross a
football team and a pig ?

Queens Pork Rangers !

What do you get if you cross a hive of bees with a
jumper knitting pattern ?

Nice and swarm !

What do you get if you cross a
fish and a deaf person ?

A herring aid !

PARDON . . .

What do you get if you cross two vicars
and a telephone line ?

A parson to parson call !

What do you get if you cross a
computer with a beefburger ?

A big mac !

What do you get if you cross a
rhinocerous with a cat ?

Very worried mice !

What do you get if you cross a sheep
with a plant ?

Cotton wool !

What do you get if you cross a sheep
with a steel bar ?

Wire wool !

What do you get if you cross a sheep
with an octopus ?

Jumpers with eight arms !

What do you get if you cross a sheep
with an outboard motor !

Baa Baa Baa Baa Baa Baa Baa Baa Baa Baa Baa Baa..

What do you get if you cross a dog
with a vegetable ?

A Jack Brussel terrier !

What do you get if you cross a sheep with a pub ?

A cocktail Baaa !

What do you get if you cross a
comedy author with a ghost ?

A crypt writer !

What do you get if you cross two
skeletons and an argument ?

A bone of contention !

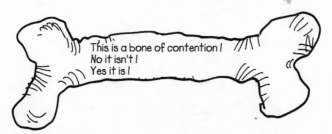

This is a bone of contention !
No it isn't !
Yes it is !

★

What do you get if you cross a witch and a
bowl of breakfast cereal ?

Snap, cackle and pop !

★

What do you get if you
cross a coat and a fire ?

A blazer !

★

What do you get if you cross a spinach eater,
a suitmaker and a hippy ?

Popeye the tailor, man !

★

What do you get if you cross a shark
and Father Christmas ?

Santa jaws !

What do you get if you cross a waiter
and a slippery floor ?

Flying saucers !

What do you get if you cross a tropical
fruit and a sad dog ?

A melon collie !

What do you get if you cross a
baby and a snake ?

A rattler !

What do you get if you cross
a chicken with a kangaroo ?

Pouched eggs !

What do you get if you cross a Star Wars
robot with a sheep ?

R 2 D ewe !

What do you get if you cross a penguin
with a hungry schoolchild ?

An empty wrapper !

What do you get if you cross a donkey with a mole ?

Mule hills in your garden !

What do you get if you cross a chicken
with a cement lorry ?

A bricklayer !

What do you get if you cross a monster and
a bowl of breakfast cereal ?

Dreaded wheat !

What do you get if you cross a bad golfer and an
outboard motor ?

Putt putt putt putt putt putt putt putt putt...

What do you get if you cross a track suit
and a tortoise ?

A shell suit !

What do you get if you cross a cat with a cushion ?

A cat a pillow !

What do you get if you cross a skeleton
and a supermodel ?

Not an ounce of fat !

What do you get if you cross a Prime Minister
and a pair of grimy spectacles ?

Blaired vision !

What do you get if you cross a Prime Minister
and a bunny ?

Blair Rabbit !

What do you get if you cross a great
invention with a herb ?

A thyme machine !

What do you get if you cross a parking
space and a camel ?

A camelot!

What do you get if you cross a half
open door and a queue of cars ?

Ajar of jam !

What do you get if you cross an
alien with a pair of gloves ?

Green fingers !

What do you get if you cross a sore throat
and some Christmas decorations ?

Tinselitis !

What do you get if you cross a turkey
with an octopus ?

A leg for everyone at Christmas dinner !

What do you get if you cross China
with a car horn ?

Hong King !

What do you get if you cross a bed with
a set of cricket wickets ?

A three poster !

What do you get if you cross a hat
with a mountain top ?

A peaked cap !

What do you get if you cross a
vegetable with a 26 mile run ?

A Marrow - thon !

What do you get if you cross a rodent and
someone who cleans your home ?

A mousekeeper !

What do you get if you cross a ghost
and a Christmas play ?

A Phantomime !

What do you get if you cross a cow with a pillar box ?

Postman cow pat !

What do you get if you cross a joke book
with an Oxo cube ?

A laughing stock !

What do you get if you cross a television
personality and a jungle animal ?

A Gnus reader !

What do you get if you cross a stick insect
and a TV presenter?

Stickolas Parsons!

What do you get if you cross a golf club
and a burrowing animal?

A mole in one!

What do you get if you cross a surgeon
and an octopus?

A doctorpus!

What do you get if you cross a robot
with a drinks machine?

C - tea - P - O!

What do you get if you cross a playing card
with a fizzy drink ?

Joker cola !

What do you get if you cross a robot with a foot ?

C - 3 - P - toe !

What do you get if you drop an iron
on someone's head ?

Hard water !

What do you get if you cross a
day of the week with buuble gum ?

Chewsday !

What do you get if you cross vampires
with some cheddar ?

Bancheese !

What do you get if you cross an
octopus with a fountain pen ?

**A squidgy pen with 8 nibs that
makes all its own ink !**

What do you get if you cross a horse with a
cake and a long rubber strip ?

A bun - gee - gee jumper !

What do you get if you cross a toad
with a science fiction film ?

Star warts !

What do you get if you cross a centipede
with a children's toy ?

**A lego, lego, lego, lego, lego, lego,...............
.lego, lego, lego, set**

What do you get if you cross a laundry basket
with a shopping basket ?

Man eating underpants !

What do you get if you cross a fairy and a turkey ?

A very strange Goblin !

What do you get if you cross a joke book
and two dozen eggs ?

A book with at least 24 yolks in it !

What do you get if you cross a fish
with a modelmaker ?

A scale model !

What do you get if you cross milk, fruit
and a scary film ?

A strawberry milk shake !

What do you get if you cross a pig
and a very old radio ?

Lots of crackling !

What do you get if you cross a
cricket ball and an alien ?

A bowling green !

What do you get if you cross a mountain
with hiccups ?

A volcano !

What athlete do you get if you cross
a snake and a sheep ?

A long jumper !

What do you get if you cross an ant and a calculator ?

An account - ant !

What do you get if you cross an army
and some babies ?

The infantry !

What do you get if
you cross a tall
building and a home
for pigs ?

A sty - scraper !

What do you get if you cross a breadcake
and a cattle rustler ?

A beef burglar !

What do you get if you cross a window
and a shirt collar ?

A pane in the neck !

What do you get if you cross a
can of oil and a mouse ?

I don't know, but at least it doesn't sqeak !

What do you get if you cross a sheep
with a discount store ?

Lots of baaaaagains !

What do you get if you cross a holidaymaker
and an elephant ?

Something that carries its own trunk !

What do you get if
you cross a camel
and a ghost ?

**Something that goes
hump in the night !**

What do you get if
you cross a ghost
and a pair
of glasses ?

Spook - tacles !

What do you get if you cross a fox
with a policeman ?

A brush with tl aw !

What do you get if you cross a feather
with a carnation ?

Tickled pink !

What do you get if you cross a spider
with a football ground ?

Webley stadium !

What do you get if you cross a boy band and some
bottles of lemonade ?

A pop group !

What do you get if you cross a chimpanzee
with an oven ?

A hairy griller !

What do you get if you cross a toad with someone
who tells strange jokes ?

Someone with a wart sense of humour !

What do you get if you cross a
jewellers shop with a boxer ?

A window full of boxing rings !

What do you get if you cross a crying baby
and a football fan ?

A footbawler !

★

What do you get if you cross an oil well
with bad manners ?

Crude oil !

★

What do you get if you cross
electricity
and a chicken ?

Battery eggs !

What do you get if you cross a fish and a birdcage ?

Perch !

What do you get if you
cross a butcher and a
dance ?

A meatball !

What do you get if you
cross a scratch
on your arm and a fruit ?

A lemon sore - bit !

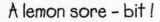

What do you get if you cross a skunk
and a winning lottery ticket ?

Stinking rich !

What do you get if you cross a ball
and a blunt instrument ?

A football club !

What do you get if you cross the sea
and a pot of chilli ?

A Mexican wave !

What do you get if you cross a donkey and a three
legged milking stool ?

A wonkey !

What do you get if you cross a sheep
and an ink cartridge ?

Something that only a sheepdog can get into a pen !

What do you get if you cross a lawn and a mat-tress ?

A flower bed !

★

What do you get if you cross a... cat with a set of water colours ?

Pusster Paints !

★

What do you get if you cross a... dog and an elephant ?

No more post !

★

What do you get if you cross a... giraffe and a dog ?

Something that bites the tyres of low flying aircraft !

★

What do you get if you cross a...
range of mountains with a dancer ?

Something huge dancing peak to peak !

What do you get if you cross a...
penguin with a paratrooper ?

A chocolate soldier !

What do you get if you cross a...
cartoon with some bubble gum ?

A carica - chewer !

What do you get if you cross a...
fox and a policeman ?

A brush with the law !

What do you get if you cross a...
pencil with window covers ?

Blinds that draw themselves !

★

What do you get if you cross a...
postman, his pet cat and a field of cows ?

Postman pat and his black and white cow pat !

What do you get if you cross a...
pig and a flea ?

Pork scratchings !

What do you get if you cross a...
Welshman and a saint ?

Good Evans !

What do you get if you cross a...
bottle of pop and a frog ?

Croaka Cola !

What do you get if you cross a...
budgie and a clown ?

Cheep and cheerful !

What do you get if you cross a...
comedian, an owl and a tube of adhesive ?

A Wit Who Glues !

What do you get if you...
pinch part of an elderly Scotsman's fish supper ?

A chip off the old Jock !

What do you get if you cross a...
field of cows and a motor boat ?

Pat pat pat pat pat pat pat pat pat.....

Awful Alphabet...

ALLOCATE

Allocate – Say hello to Kate !

A

Abandon - When a pop group is playing !

Abrade -   A Chinese knife !

Accident -   When you cut yourself chopping firewood !

Address -   Something a woman wears at her wedding !

Adorn -   A beautiful start to the day !

Aftermath - The result of a catastrophe - is where we get the word maths !

Airliner - The person who paints the lines down the side of Jumbo jets!

Allocate - Say hello to Kate !

Antelope - When two ants run off to get married !

Antifreeze - When your Mum's sister goes out without a coat in Winter !

Arrest - What a burglar gets when he goes to bed !

Automate - A robot for a best pal !

B

Bacteria - The rear entrance to a cafeteria !

Bandage - The average age of a pop group !

Banshee - Don't let that ghost in here !

Barber - Sheep trained as a hairdresser !

Bark - The sound made by a wooden dog !

Bateau - What the French use to play tenniso, squasho and cricketo !

Batman - The secret identity of Dracula !

Beauty Spot - When flowers grow out of your head !

Berth - Where they keep any babies born at sea !

Beverage - Slightly worse than average !

Beware - What bees wear, of course !

Bichromate - A friend you go cycling with !

C

Cabbage - How old a taxi is !

Cagoule - Ghost who goes around in a car !

Canary Islands - Where cats like to go for
their holidays !

Candidate -   The sweets you take to impress
a new girlfriend !

Capacity -   The size of your head !

Carousel - A used car dealership !

Carrot - Rust !

Chemistry - The tree you end up in when the lab explodes !

Chipmunk - Chef in a monastery !

Clay Pigeon - School dinners !

Commentator - Any potato that isn't a Jersey Royal or King Edward !

Crime Wave - Where robbers go to surf !

Czeck - Money paid into a foreign bank account !

D

Debate - De thing on de fish hook !

Defeatist - Someone who designs shoes !

Demijohn - Robin Hood's best friend !

Dentist - Car body repairer !

Descant - Ant that lives in a school !

Desert - Pudding made from sand !

Detention - The fear of being kept behind at school!

Diplomat - A mat for kneeling on when you meet a V.I.P.!

Discount - How much a shop assistant will knock off a new CD player 'cos he's no good at maths!

Distressed - Having all your hair cut off!

Dynamo - Welshman refusing to cut the grass!

E

Earring -   Answer the telephone !

Eclipse -   Hedge cutter !

Editor -   Policeman's truncheon !

Eider -   Not bothered !

Einstein - One glass of beer !

Elastic Band - A group who play rubber instruments !

Electrocute - Pretty electrician !

Engineers - Ears on an engine !

Extension - More stress caused by a longer exam !

F

Factory - The place where they make trees !

Falter - Give a girl low marks in a test !

Fax - The truth !

Feedback - A baby being sick !

Fez - Nickname for a pheasant !

Fiddlesticks - Violin bows !

Figure Head - Someone who is good at maths !

Finishing School - The start of the Summer holidays !

Fish and chips - What they serve in the canteen of a nuclear power station !

Flash bulb - A light bulb that thinks very highly of itself !

Footnote - When you try to hide a five pound note with your shoe, until no-one is looking and you can pick it up !

Frankincense - The man who runs the perfume shop !

G

Game keeper – The teacher who confiscates your Nintendo !

Gazette – Baby Gazelle !

Germinate – Bacteria in bad food !

Genealogy – Finding out if there is a genie in your family history !

Glacier – The cold stare of the man fixing the windows you smashed with your football !

Gymkhana – The owner of the local riding school !

H

Hail stones - Over cooked water droplets !

Hallmarks - Black skid marks on the corridor you make as you screech to a halt when a teacher comes round the corner suddenly !

Handiwork - A job just around the corner from where you live !

Hatchback - A car full of baby chicks !

Headrest - Lunch time !

Heirloom -   When someone leaves you a pet rabbit in their will !

Hemlock -   Special stitch used around the bottom of a skirt !

Highway Code -   What hitch hikers catch from standing about in the rain !

Hippodrome – Where hippos go to learn to fly !

Honey comb –   What bees use to style their hair !

Hot Cross Bun – What you get if you pour boiling
water down a rabbit hole !

I

Ice lolly - What they use for money at the North Pole !

Icicle - A bicycle with a bit missing !

Ideogram - Telegram sent to an idiot !

Ignite - Eskimo's bedtime !

Impatient - Someone fidgeting in the doctor's waiting room !

Implicate - Blame Kate for something she didn't do !

Infant -   Baby elephant !

Infantry -   Army made up of baby elephants !

Infiltrate - Sneaking Phil into the football match
               without paying !

Instep -   The latest dance !

Instrumental -   Driven crazy by next door's
                      piano lessons !

J

Jackdaw - Small entrance for birds found in a tree!

Jam packed - A very full sandwich!

Jargon - Stolen jar!

Jitterbug - Insect that can't sit still!

Joan of Arc - Noah's wife!

Jodhpurs - Trousers worn by a cat !

Juggernaut - Empty jug !

K

Kaleidoscope – Bump into people while you're looking through a telescope !

Ketchup – Run as fast as a bottle of sauce !

Kettle drum – What the orchestra uses to make a cup of tea !

Kipper – Sleeping fish !

Knickers -   Burglars !

Knit wear -   Jumper for a fool !

L

Labrador - Dog that helps a scientist with his experiments !

Lacewing - Where prisoners make lace !

Lactose - Monster with ends of feet cut off !

Lambda - Greek letter invented by a sheep !

Lamination - Country ruled by sheep !

Lassitude - Monster eats girl !

Laughing Stock - What you get if you tickle an Oxo cube !

Launderette - A small launder - but I've no idea what a launder is !?

Leek - Vegetable that is not allowed on a boat !

Lemonade - What you give a deaf orange !

Leopard Lilly - A plant you should never sniff !

Level Headed -   What you will be if someone drops a car on your head !

Lie Detector -   What sneaky teachers use to see who is asleep in the class !

Light Fingered - Someone who steals bulbs !

Lockjaw - What you are likely to get if you swallow a bunch of keys !

Logarithm - Music played by pieces of wood !

Loose Leaf Folder - Where to store all the fallen Autumn leaves !

Luke warm - What Luke is every winter because he manages to sit next to the only radiator in the class room !

Luminous - Toilets that glow in the dark !

M

Macintosh - Waterproof Computer !

Magician - Anyone who can score more than 14% in a maths examination !

Magneto - Italian for magnet !

Mammoth - Large hairy moth with tusks - now extinct !

Manure -   What some odd people put on their rhubarb - I put custard on mine !

Marionette - Marion's little sister !

Marksman - Teacher with exam results file !

Marxist -   Someone who watches old Marx Brothers films all day !

Melancholy -   What you get if you cross a sheep dog with a fruit !

Mental Block - When someone stands in front of the door in the exam room to stop you escaping !

Metacarpus - Scene of an accident involving a motor vehicle and a cat !

Metronome - Short person working on the Paris underground railway system !

Minimum - Metronome's mother !

Mumbo Jumbo - Elephant who doesn't speak clearly !

MUMBLE...
MUTTER...

Mushroom - The room where all the Eskimos go to train their husky dogs to pull sleds. You will often hear the word 'mush' as you walk past !

Mute - A Lute without any strings !

N

Nag - Tell off a horse !

Nappy - Liable to fall asleep in History lessons !

Negligent - Man in a nightie !

Newsagent - Spy hiding behind a newspaper !

Nickname - Put someone else's name on your exam paper !

Nightmare - Horse that can only be ridden during the hours of darkness !

Nipper - Baby crab !

Nose Cone - Trip up and splat the end of your ice cream into your face !

Nuclear Fuel - Someone who messes around in a power station !

O

Oblique - The feeling you get at the start of a three hour maths exam !

Oblong - The feeling you get when you have finished all the questions and it is still only half way through a three hour maths exam !

Octangle - The feeling an octopus gets in a three hour maths exam !

Offenbach - Noisy dog !

Offensive - Garden fence that nobody likes !

Opt out - Leave the sports field because of a damaged foot !

Orchid - Baby orchestra !

Orienteering - Trying to find your way to Asia with out a map or compass !

Outcrop - That little tuft of hair that the barber always seems to miss !

Outnumber - Finally leaving that three hour maths exam !

P

Padlocks - handcuffs for cats and dogs !

Pamphlet - Leaflet written by Pam !

Pant - Half a pair of trousers !

Paranoid - Robot who is convinced that someone is out to get him !

Parasite - Where leeches go on their Summer holiday !

Parking Meter - Space for a very, very short car !

Parrot Fashion - What trendy parrots wear !

Part Exchange - Transplant surgery !

Party Wall - What neighbours bang on when you make too much noise !

Pas de Deux - Less than 2% in the French Exam !

Picket - What you do when your nose goes on strike !

Pigment - Special paint for colouring pigs !

Q

Quadrangle - Fight in the school playground !

Quadratic Equation - Maths problem that you need at least 4 people to solve !

Quasimodo - Don't remember the name, but the face rings a bell !

Quicksilver - Easily spent pocket money !

R

Raquet - Noise made by tennis players !

Rainbow - What the rain wears in its hair !

Ransome - Only completed part of the school cross country race !

Ransome Note - A letter that someone gives the teacher to tell him that you only ran part of the cross country !

Ratbag – Mouse's rucksack !

Ray Gun – Previous President of the United States !

Recycle – Do up an old bike !

Rehearse – Drive back to the graveyard !

Remainder – All the numbers you are left with at the end of the maths exam !

Reverse Charge – Who you telephone to stop a herd of wild elephants !

Roller Skate - Sea fish with his own wheels !

Rosette - Small rose !

Royal Blue - When the Queen is fed up !

Rubber Tree - What the use to make those pencils with an eraser at the end !

Rustle - Paper boy !

S

Salad Dressing - What you will see salad do when it gets up in the morning !

Sand Bank - Where camels keep their savings !

Satire - Sitting in a tall chair !

Scatter Cushions - Result of a pillow fight !

Scholastic - What holds up your P.E. shorts !

Schumaker - cobbler !

Scissors - Swimming leg action designed to cut through the water !

Scotch Egg - What you get if you feed chickens whisky !

Scrunch - Lunchbox run over by a bus !

Sea Horse - What the idiot bought because he wanted to play water polo !?

Semiconductor - Part time bus driver !

Shamrock - A plant pretending to be a stone !

Sheba - Queen with a lot of sheep !

Sheep Dip - What wolves have at parties !

Sheep Dog Trial - What happens after sheep dogs are arrested !

Sheet Lightning - What happens if lightning hits your bed !

Shellfish - Crustaceans that never share anything !

Shingle - How a drunk asks for one !

Shortbread - A loaf cut in half !

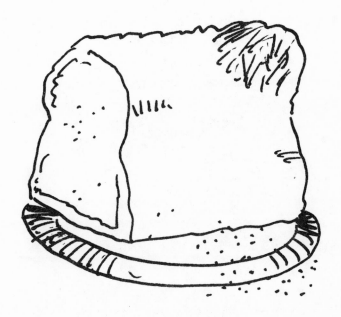

Spell Checker - Computer software for witches !

T

Tactical - Tickling a small nail !

Tap Dancer - Someone trying to do River Dance in the sink !

Telethon - Well, Thwitch it off then Thilly !

Tinfoil - Not very thick foil !

Tirade - Robbery in a tie shop !

Toadstool - Hammer belonging to a toad !

Toulouse - Two toilets !

Track Suit - What a railway line wears when it goes out jogging !

Traffic Jam - What policemen have in their sandwiches !

Tycoon - Someone who has made a lot of money selling ties !

U

Ultimatum - When you tell your friend for the last time !

Umpire - Vampire who can't spell !

Unaware - Boxer shorts !

Undecided - Not knowing what colour unaware to put on !

Underpass - Handing secret notes under your desk !

Underrate - Any number from 1 to 7

Unit - Fool !

University - Training school for poets !

Unleaded - Empty pencil case !

Unstable - Horse that lives in a field !

V

Vacuum Cleaner - Used to keep outer space nice and tidy !

Vague - (Sorry, not sure about this one !)

Vampire - Where you go to hire a vamp !

Varnish - A posh way of disappearing !

Vespers - Very quiet whispers !

Vest - opposite to East !

W

Waist Coat - *Jacket made from scraps of material !*

Wardrobe - *Cupboard that joins the army !*

Warhead -
Head
teacher
who joins
the army !
Hurrah !

Warren -
A man who
keeps pet
rabbits !

Weight Watcher - *Someone who spend a lot of time looking at their tum !*

X - Y - Z

X-Ray - Used to belong to Ray !

Xylophone - What aliens from the planet Xylo use to telephone each other !

Yak - What you say when you stand in something nasty !

Yam - How they say Jam in Holland !

Yardstick - Sweeping brush with a missing head !

Yellow Hammer - What you shout when you hit your thumb !

Yellow Pages - Homework book with tea spilled on it !

Yoga - Cartoon bear !

Yokel - Farmworker who paints egg yolks yellow !

Zebra - Mobile road crossing !

Zermatt - What you wipe zer feet on !

Zinc - Where you wash your hands !

Zing - What you do with zongs in a choir !

Zoo - What a solicitor does !

Zoom Lens - The sound of a camera falling from a great height !

Zulu - The toilets in the zoo !

Hospital Howls...

Doctor, doctor...
my son is turning into a cricket bat !

Hmm ! Well, this has got me stumped !

Why did the angry doctor have to retire ?

Because he had lost all his patients !

Doctor, doctor...
I think I've got an inferiority complex !

No you haven't - you really are inferior !

★

Ah. Mr Smith, have your eyes ever been checked ?

No doctor, they've always been blue !

Doctor, doctor...
There's a man to see you with a wooden leg called
Jenkins.

What's his other leg called ?

Doctor, doctor...
I think I'm turning into a
wasp !

**Hmm , give me a buzz if
things get really bad !**

Doctor, doctor...
I've just been stung by a
wasp !

Did you put anything on it ?

**No, he seemed to enjoy it
just as it was !**

★

Doctor, doctor...
I've got an itchy spotty patch on my nose,
should I put cream on it ?

Now, now, let's not do anything rash !

★

Doctor, doctor...
I've not stopped laughing since my operation !

Well, I told you the surgeon would have you in stitches !

Doctor, doctor...
I've got pigeon toes !

**Don't worry we'll find a suitable tweetment for you...
but for now just put this birdseed in your shoes !**

Doctor, doctor...
My belly is so big I'm embarrassed by it !

Have you tried to diet ?

Yes, but whatever colour I use it still sticks out !

Doctor's Bookcase...

TRAINING TO BE A SURGEON

by

I. CUTTEM – OPEN

Doctor, doctor...
I feel like a twenty pound note !

Go shopping, the change will do you good !

Doctor, doctor...
I can't stop shoplifting !

Try taking two of these pills every morning,
and if that doesn't work bring me
a CD player next week !

Doctor, doctor...
Did you hear about the appendix who
went out and bought a new suit -
because he heard that the doctor was
going to take him out !

Doctor, doctor...
Which king was also a doctor ?

William the corn curer !

Doctor, doctor...
Is it true that you can get pills to improve your memory?

Of course you can, how many would you like?

How many what?

Doctor, doctor...
Which kings needed medical attention?

**Charles the sick
and
Henry the ache!**

Doctor, doctor...
I feel as sick as a dog !

I'll make an appointment for you to see a vet !

Doctor, doctor...
Thank you for coming - I'm at death's door !

Don't worry, I'll pull you through !

Doctor, doctor...
What can I do to help me get to sleep ?

Have you tried counting sheep ?

Yes, but then I have to wake up to drive home again !

Doctor, doctor...
I've got a terrible cough !

Well you should practice more !

Doctor, doctor...
After the operation on my hand
will I be able to play the piano ?
Of course you will Mr Smith !

Great - because I never could before !

Doctor, doctor...
my son is turning into a cricket bat !

Hmm ! Well, this has got me stumped !

Doctor, doctor...
I think I'm turning into a fish !

Well, just hop up on to the scales !

Doctor, doctor...
I feel like a goat !

Really - and how are the kids ?

★

Doctor, doctor...
I think I'm turning into a bridge !

Really - what's come over you ?

Doctor, doctor...
Why did the chemist tell everyone to be quiet ?

Because she didn't want to wake the sleeping pills !

Doctor, doctor...
These tablets you gave me last week seem
to get smaller every day ?!

Yes, they're slimming pills !

Doctor, doctor...
I think I'm turning into a toad !

Don't worry, we can do an hoperation
for that these days !

★

Doctor, doctor...
Can you put me in touch with the local plastic surgeon ?

I'm afraid not, he sat too close to the
radiator last night and melted !

Doctor, doctor...
I have a fish hook stuck in the side of my mouth !

**I thought you were waiting to see me
with baited breath !**

Doctor, doctor...
I've just been stung by a giant wasp !

I'll give you some cream to put on it !

Don't be daft - it'll be miles away by now !

Doctor, doctor...
My new job at the laundry is very tiring !

I thought you looked washed out !

Ah. Mr Blenkinsop. Did you drink the medicine
I gave you after your bath?

No, Doctor, I couldn't even drink all the bath
let alone the medicine!

Doctor, doctor...
I get a lot of headaches from my wooden leg.

Why is that?

Because my wife keeps hitting me
over the head with it!

Doctor, doctor...
I think I have a split personality!

I'd better give you a second opinion then!

Doctor, doctor...
I got trampled by a load of cows!

So I herd!

Doctor, doctor...
I keep imagining I,m a sunken ship and it's
really got me worried!

Sounds to me like you're a nervous wreck!

Doctor, doctor...
My snoring wakes me up every night!

Try sleeping in another bedroom, then you
won't be able to hear it!

Doctor, doctor...
I feel quite like my old self again!

Oh Dear, I better put you back on the tablets then!

Doctor, doctor...
I think I have acute appendicitis!

Yes, it is rather nice isn't it!

Doctor, doctor...
My hair is falling out - can you give me something to
keep it in ?

Here's a paper bag ?!

Doctor, doctor...
What can you give me for my kidneys ?

How about a pound of onions ?!

Doctor, doctor...
I've fractured my elbow bone !

Humerus ?

Well, I don't think it's particularly funny !

Doctor, doctor...
Is this disease contagious ?

Not at all !

Then why are you standing out on the window ledge ?!

Doctor, doctor...
You don't really think I'm turning into a
grandfather clock do you ?

No, I was just winding you up !

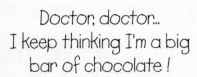

Doctor, doctor...
I keep thinking I'm a big
bar of chocolate !

**Come and sit here, and
don't worry, I won't
bite - I'm just a big old
pussycat really !**

Grim Giggles...

What do you call an overweight vampire?

Draculard!

What do monsters eat for breakfast ?

Human beans on toast !

How many skeletons can you fit in an empty coffin ?

Just one - after that it's not empty any more !

What did the *mummy* ghost say to the little ghost ?

Don't spook until you're spooken to !

★

Where would you find a suitable gift for
a tortured ghost ?

In a chain store !

What kind of ice cream do vampires like best ?

Necktarine flavour !

Why did the vampire bite a computer ?

He wanted to get onto the interneck !

What day of the week do vampires and werewolves like best ?

Moonday - especially full-moonday !

What sort of ghost would you find up your nose ?

A Bogeyman !

How do you know if there is a ghost in a hotel ?

Ask to see the hotel in - spectre !

Why should you never run if you see a werewolf ?

Because they go mad for fast food !

What sort of music do ghosts like best ?

Haunting melodies !

How do mummies go into their pyramids ?

Gift wrapped !

Why did the zombie go to the chemists ?

He wanted something to stop his coffin !

How do you get a mummy interested in music ?

Play him some wrap !

What should you never order if you're
eating out with a vampire ?

Steak and chips !

What is a ghosts' favourite creature ?

The Whale !

Why do ghosts go back to the same place
every year for their holidays ?

They like their old haunts best !

Vampire Hunters Menu. . .

GARLIC BREAD

followed by

HAMMERED STEAK

and finally

HOT CROSS BUNS

What do you call a ghost that doesn't scare anyone ?

A failure !

What does a well brought up vampire say
after he has bitten your neck ?

Fang you very much !

VAMPIRE SAYINGS...

Once bitten - twice bitten !

A neck in your hand is worth two in a bush !

A stitch in time - means I can come back for some more !

There's many a slip twixt neck and lip !

What is a skeleton ?

A body with the person scraped off !

What does a skeleton feed his dog ?

Anything but bones !!

Why do skeletons take a dog with them to the seaside ?

They need something to bury them in the sand !

★

Why do skeletons drink lots of milk ?

Because calcium is good for your bones !

What do skeletons eat on Good Friday ?

Hot Cross Bones !

Why do skeletons dislike horror films ?

Because they scare them to the marrow !

What sort of jokes do skeletons enjoy ?

Rib ticklers !

What do skeletons sing at
birthday parties ?

Femur jolly good fellow. . .

Why was the skeleton's jacket
in shreds ?
Because he had very sharp
shoulder blades !

What do skeleton schoolchildren wear ?

Knee caps !

What do vampires eat at parties ?

Fang Furters !

What do you call a very old vampire ?

A Gran-pire !

How do vampires and ghosts go on holiday ?

By Scareyplane !

What did the teacher say to the naughty vampires in class ?

Stop Dracularking about !

Did you hear about the ghost who cut down trees at three o'clock in the morning ?

He was the thing that made stumps in the night !

What do you call twin ghosts ?

Dead ringers !

★

Why was the vampire lying dead on the floor of the restaurant ?

It was a steak house !

What does a young boy ghost do to get a girlfriend ?

He woooooooos her !

What are the only jobs that skeletons can get ?

Skeleton staff !

What about the two ghosts who got married - it was love at first fright !

What do ghosts do if they are afraid ?

Hide under a sheet !

What is the difference between a ghost
and a custard cream biscuit ?

Have you tried dipping a ghost in your tea ?!

How does a skeleton know when it's going to rain ?

He just gets a feeling in his bones !

What is ... visible - invisible - visible - invisible - visible -
invisible ?

A skeleton on a zebra crossing !

Where do vampires get washed ?

In the bat room !

What room must all werewolf homes have ?

A changing room !

What sort of shampoo do ghosts use ?

Wash and Groan !

Why did the skull go to the disco on his own ?

He had no body to go with !

★

GHASTLY GHOSTLY SAYINGS...

Two's company - threes a shroud !

Never kick a ghost while he's down -
your foot will just go through him !

He who laughs last - obviously hasn't
seen the ghost standing behind him !

What do ghosts watch on TV ?

Scare Trek !

Horror Nation Street !

Bone and Away !

The Booos at Ten !

Sesame Sheet !

Have I got whoooos for you !

and, of course...

Till Death Us Do Part !

What can you use to flatten a ghost ?
A spirit level !

Why did the ghosts have a party ?

They wanted to lift their spirits !

What do ghosts carry their luggage in
when they go on holiday ?

Body bags !

SKELEMENU...

Ox-Tail Soup

followed by

Spare Ribs and Finger Buffet

finishing with

Marrowbone Jelly and Custard !

What do skeletons learn about at school ?

Decimals and Fractures !

★

Where does a vampire keep his money ?

In a blood bank !

★

What do you call an overweight vampire ?

Draculard !

★

What do you call a vampire who has been in the pub ?

Drunkula !

What do you call a vampire that hides in the kitchen?

Spatula!

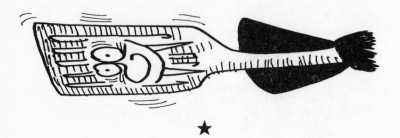

★

What do you call a vampire mummy?

Wrapula!

What do you call a young vampire?

Draculad!

What do you call a vampire that attacks insects?

A cricket bat!

Mad Martians...

How often do you find toilets in space?

Once in a loo moon!

Why didn't the Martian have his
birthday party on the Moon?

There was no atmosphere!

What is soft and sweet and fluffy
and comes from Mars?

BUT HOW ARE WE GOING TO EAT THEM!?*

A Mars-mallow!

What do astronauts have in their packed lunch?

Launcheon Meat!

What do astronauts wear when it's cold ?

Apollo neck jumpers !

How do you know that Saturn is married ?

You can see the ring !

What game do bored Aliens play ?

Astro noughts and crosses !

Why did the space monster cover his rocket
with tomato sauce ?

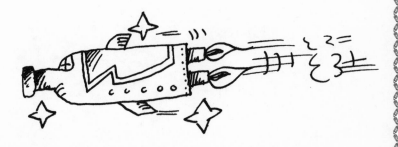

So the nasty aliens couldn't ketchup with him !

What do the aliens from the planet Skunkus ride in ?

Phew F O's !

When the alien picked up his brand new spaceship he was
really pleased - he'd never had a **NEW F O** before !

What sort of spaceships do aliens from the planet Footwear use ?

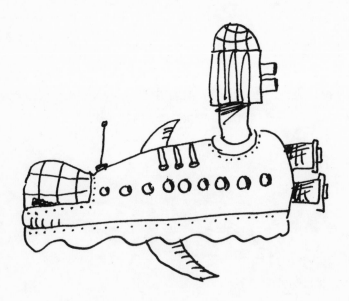

Shoe F O's

How did the space aliens go into the space ark ?

R 2 D 2 by R 2 D 2 !

★

Alien - Beware Earthling, I could eat your entire planet !

Blenkinsop - **That's nothing, yesterday I ate an entire Galaxy !**

★

What do you call a pub on Mars ?

A Mars bar !

★

Why did the spaceship land outside your bedroom ?

I must have left the landing light on !

What do you call a space creature that
doesn't pass his space exams?

A Fail-ien!

What do you get in an alien transport cafe?

Unidentified frying objects!

What is the smallest space explorer called?

A Mouse-tronaut!

What do space ramblers like to do?

Go on Star Treks!

What do you never get if you cross a
bug eyed alien with a dog?

Burgled!

What is the first thing an alien puts on
when he gets out of bed?

His feet - ON - the floor!

Where do aliens keep their sandwiches?

In a launch box!

Why are aliens good gardeners?

They have green fingers!

Knock, knock...
Who's there ?
Jupiter.
Jupiter who ?
Jupiter space ship on my front lawn ?!

What goes in one year and out the other ?

A time machine !

If astronauts breathe oxygen during the day,
what do they breathe at night ?

Nitrogen !

Knock, knock...
Who's there ?
Saturn.
Saturn who ?
Saturn front of this spaceship
waiting for take off time !

What is the weakest part of space called ?

The Punyverse !

What robots are made from small planets ?

Aster - droids !

What do you call a vampire version of Star Trek ?

The Necks Generation !

Human –   Why have you got holes in your hand ?

Alien –   I have been using the computer.

Human –   But that's not dangerous !?

Alien –   **Maybe not on Earth, but on my planet when we talk about computer bytes we mean something different !**

Why do creatures from the planet THaaarRRgh wear slimy green braces ?

To hold their slimy green trousers up !

What do you call a glass robot ?

See through P O !

Why couldn't the moon eat any more supper ?

Because it was full !

What teddy bear story do robot children read at bedtime ?

Tinny - the - Pooh !

What does the alien hairdresser do when the shadow of the earth obscures the sun ?

Eclipse !

How do you get a baby alien to sleep ?

Rocket !

What did the grape say when the space monster trod on him ?

Nothing - he just let out a little whine !

What do you call a noisy space ship ?

A space racket !

What do space aliens watch on TV ?

Countdown !

Why is the letter V like a space monster ?

Because it comes after you !

What do you call the planet that is inhabited solely by impressionists ?

Planet of the apes !

Which part of a space suit is German ?

The Helmut !

Which Egyptian King was named after a planet ?

Tutankhamoon !

Why are alien kitchens always such a mess ?

Because of all the flying sauces !

What did the tree alien say when he landed on Earth ?

Take me to your Cedar !

What would you do if you saw a spaceman ?

Park in it, man !

Why did the alien buy a twisted spaceship ?

He wanted to travel at warp speed !

Why couldn't the idiot's spaceship travel
at the speed of light ?

Because he took off in the dark !

What do you call dishonest spaceships ?

Lying saucers !

What sort of spaceships do secret agents fly in ?

Spying saucers !

What do you call miserable spaceships ?

Sighing saucers !

Which space villain looks like a pair of wellies ?

Darth Waders !

How often do you find toilets in space ?

Once in a loo moon !

Where do you leave your spaceship whilst you visit another planet ?

At a parking meteor !

What sort of music do space aliens like best ?

Rocket and roll !

and

Heavy Metal !

Where do they lock up naughty space creatures ?

Jailien !

Why does Captain Kirk make the crew
clean the Enterprise ?

He Likes things Spock and span !

Where do you sometimes hear singing in space ?

When you fly past a pop star !

Why did the alien build a spaceship from feathers ?

He wanted to travel light years !

Did you hear about the alien poet -
she wrote universes !

Why did Captain Kirk shave his head ?

To baldly go where no-one had been before !

Did you hear about the silly alien who
built a spaceship from herbs ?

He wanted to travel in thyme !

What do alien footballers wear when
they arrive on Earth ?

Their landing strip !

What fast food do computers eat ?

Ram Burgers !

What piece of sports equipment does every alien own ?

A tennis rocket !

Why did the alien take a nuclear missile to the party ?

In case he fancied blowing up some balloons !

Did you hear about the fat alien - he had to wear a
'not very much' space suit!

Odds & Ends...

Why are you taking that shovel to your
singing class?

So I can get to the low notes!

What do you call an underwater spy?

James Pond!

What sort of dancing will elephants
do in your front room?

Break dancing!

Knock, knock...
Who's there?
Boo.
Boo who?

No need to get upset, it's just a game!

Where would you find a rubber trumpet ?

In an elastic band !

What time is it when you have
eaten half of your lunch ?

Half ate !

Doctor, doctor...
I feel like the man in the moon !

What has come over you ?
A cow !

What sort of car is a Rolls-Canardly?

A car that rolls down hills
but can hardly get up them!

What is a duck filled fatty puss?

An overweight cat that has just eaten a duck!

How do electricians get over high fences?

They volt!

I asked for vegetarian sausage -
these are made from beef !

But the cow was a vegetarian !

Where does Father Christmas go
for his Summer holidays ?

Santa Maria !

Hello, Carol, how was your first day at school ?

First - you mean I have to go back again ?!

Did you hear about the cowboy who used to sit up all
night making models of cows from tissue paper - he
was sacked for rustling !

A man ran into a bar and got three fractured ribs...

...it was a steel bar !

A man wanted to be a lumberjack...
He flew out to Canada and bought a chainsaw and got a job. At the end of the first week he had cut down 100 trees. 'That's not enough,' said the foreman, 'we expect you to cut down at least 200.'
However, he offered to buy the man's chainsaw to help with his air fare home.
"I'll just test it first,' said the foreman, and started the engine.
'How do you get it to make that noise?' said the man !?

When do you change the water in a goldfish bowl ?

When they've drunk the first lot !

What do ghosts shout at a bad play ?

Boooooooooooo !

What do skeletons say after they've
seen a really good play?

That was a rattling good show!

How does Jack Frost get about?

By Icycle!

★

What do you call a travel agent in the jungle?

A Trip - opotamus!

What drink do Autralian bear manufacture ?

Coca - Koala !

Which animal tells the best jokes ?

A stand -up chameleon !

What's the quickest way to get out of the jungle ?

By ele - copter !

What sort of poetry is known everywhere ?

Uni - verse !

My Dad must be the greatest magician ever - yesterday he turned his car into a side street, and the day
before he turned it into a lay-by !

Waiter - where's *my* elephant sandwich ?

Sorry, Sir, I forgot !

What do bogey men drink ?

Demon - ade !

Who do female ghouls get married to ?

Edible batchelors !

What prize is awarded each year to the best dieter ?

The *No* - Belly Prize !

Nurse - can you take this patient's temperature please ?

Certainly doctor - where to ?

Why are you taking that shovel to your singing class ?

So I can get to the low notes !

Before you give anyone a piece of your mind -
check to make sure you will have enough
left for yourself afterwards !

What's round, shiny, smelly and comes out at night ?

A foul moon !

Does Cyclops get a television licence at half price ?

Are my indicators working ?

On and off !

Why is that farmer setting fire
to the plants in his field ?

He's growing baked beans !

Why did you give up your job as a fortune teller ?

To be honest I couldn't see any future in it !

How do you know if a Boa-constrictor loves you ?

It will have a crush on you !

Why do boxers like going to parties ?

They love to get to the punch !

How do you know where an
escaped train is hiding ?

Just follow the tracks !

What sort of boats do clever
schoolchildren travel on ?

Scholar - ships !

Who runs the pub in the jungle ?

The wine-ocerous !

Knock, knock...
Who's there ?
Alison.
Alison who ?
Alison to you asking me that question every day !

Knock, knock...
Who's there ?
Alpaca.
Alpaca who ?
Alpaca suitcase and leave if you keep
asking these silly questions !

What do you get if the central heating goes
haywire in a pet shop ?

Hot dogs !

What game do prisoners like best ?

Cricket - they like to hit and run !

Which vegetable is best at snooker ?

The Cue - cumber !

What do you call a man who preserves pears ?

Noah !

What did the artists say when he had to
choose a pencil ?

2B or not 2B, that is the question !

How do you know when your dustbin is
full of toadstools ?

Because there's not mushroom inside !

What do you get if you cross a cow with a monster ?

A horrible mootation !

Why did the stick insect cover himself with marmite ?

He was going to a fancy dress party as a twiglet !

Which ancient leader invented the cruet set ?

Sultan pepper !

Is that bacon I smell ?

It is and you do !

What is a robot's favourite snack?

Nucler fission Microchips!

What do you do with a ladder in
a hot country?

Climate!

What runs round the garden without
ever getting out of breath?

The fence!

What do you call a man who looks at the
sky all night long?

A night watchman!

What animal lives on your head ?

The hare !

Did you hear about the robot policeman ?

He was a PC - PC !

And - did you hear about the mechanical writer ?

Robot Louis Stevenson !

Where do monsters go fishing ?

Goole !

Why did the idiot try to spread a goat on his toast ?

Because someone told him it was a butter !

Where should you send a one-legged,
short sighted man ?

To the hoptician !

What do you get if you cross a bird with a frog ?

Pigeon toed !

What is the difference between a mad rabbit
and a forged £50 note ?

One is a mad bunny, the other is bad money !

Doctor, are you sure it's my arteries that
are the problem ?

Listen I'm a doctor, aorta know !

When is a King like a book ?

When he has lots of pages !

★

Why did the jelly wobble ?

Because it saw the milk shake !

★

Water –   A colourless liquid that turns brown
           when you put your hands into it !

★

Why did the idiots stand in an open doorway ?

They wanted to play draughts !

Why didn't the idiot's home made airbag stop him from breaking his nose when he crashed ?

He didn't have enough time to blow it up !

Where do very tough posties sleep ?

On pillow boxes !

Why were the judge and jury on a boat ?

Because the prisoner was in the dock !

What sort of food is made from old Chinese boats ?

Junk food !

★

What do you call a happy crocodile with a camera ?

Snap happy !

★

Why are so many famous artists French ?

Because they were born in France !

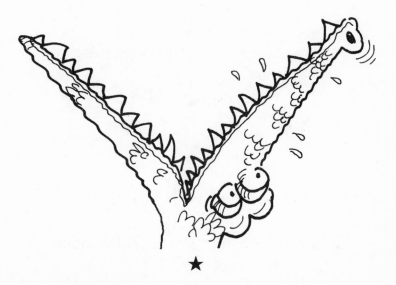

★

Why did the American Indian chief put
smokeless fuel on the fire ?

He wanted to send some secret messages !

What did the paper say to the pencil ?

You lead me astray !

Why do wolves howl at the moon ?

Because they have such rotten singing voices !

What goes up a drainpipe down but
can't come down a drainpipe up ?

An Umbrella !

Did you hear about the man who drove round telling everyone he was rich and successful, when he was actually a failure ?

He was a mobile phoney !

Why was the poor dog chasing his tail ?

He was trying to make ends meet !

How do you know when you come to the end of a joke book ?

Because there's no more laughing matter !

389